Cape Verde Islands

Front cover: Vale do Paúl, Santo Antão

Right: Vila do Maio

TOP 10 ATTRACTIONS

Carnival. Noise, colour, glitter and feathers add up to an unforgettable celebration, at its best in Mindelo. See page 66.

Praia de Santa Maria. A beach of dazzling white sand on Sal, perfect for watersports. See page 30.

Fajã d'Água. A stunningly situated village on Brava, one of the country's smallest and prettiest islands. See page 64.

Fontainhas. An impossibly picturesque mountain village on Santo Antão reached by a winding coastal road. See page 74.

Parque Natural do Fogo. Cape Verde's only live volcano, Pico do Fogo, is a perfect cone of lava and ash. See page 58.

Vale do Paúl. Lush, green hiking country on Santo Antão, bursting with tropical fruit trees. See page 74.

Cidade Velha. The cradle of Cape Verdean society on Santiago, with a fort and ruins to explore. See page 52.

Mindelo. The capital of São Vicente is an invigorating place to experience café culture, island-style. See page 65.

Parque Natural de Monte Gordo. A unique mountain region in the shadow of a mighty extinct volcano on São Nicolau. See page 80.

Deserto de Viana. Enormous drifts of beautiful, shifting sand, accumulated on Boa Vista over millennia. See page 39.

A PERFECT TOUR

Day 1 **Santa Maria**

Head for Santa Maria and spend half a day at the sandy Praia de Santa Maria beach, sunbathing and swimming in the turquoise water. In the afternoon take a stroll in the village, watch the fishermen unload their catch at the Pontão jetty, then enjoy a relaxed dinner at a local restaurant.

Day 3 **Boa Vista**

Fly to Boa Vista, then hire a 4x4 and go off-roading amidst picturesque shifting dunes and extinct volcanoes. Visit the small, cosy town of Sal Rei and watch Cape Verdeans playing *oril*, the local version of the game of holes and seeds.

Day 4 **Mindelo**

Fly to São Vicente. On arrival in São Pedro's aerodrome, check out the monument to the São Vicente-born "Barefoot Diva," Cesária Évora. Stroll the cobblestone streets of Mindelo and admire the colourful merchants' houses, and be sure to grab a snack at the hippest place in town, Café Mindelo.

Day 2 **Ponta Preta and Pedra de Lume**

If you're into surfing, head for Ponta Preta, Cape Verde's most famous windsurfing location, slightly northwest of Santa Maria. Alternatively, hire a car and drive to the east coast to the Salinas at Pedra de Lume's, a rudimentary saltwater spa in an extinct volcanic crater. Float effortlessly on the salty water and treat yourself to a relaxing massage.

IN CAPE VERDE

Praia

Fly to the capital Praia, on Santiago, for a day of history and culture. Visit the Museu Etnográfico to see some magnificent examples of *pano* weaving and the Museu de Arqueologia for an exhibition of shipwreck salvage. After sunset head to the legendary music venue, Quintal de Música, to hear local music at its best.

Day 8 **Fogo**

Fly to Fogo, take in São Filipe's lovely colonial houses and *sobrados*, then head by car for Chã das Caldeiras in Parque Natural do Fogo, to taste local wine and dine on fresh fish. From Fogo fly back to Sal.

Day 5 **Santo Antão**

Hop on a ferry from Mindelo to Santo Antão. The only truly green island in Cape Verde, it boasts spectacular valleys and hills. Enjoy a day's hiking or go on a mountain bike tour with an experienced guide. In the evening, take the ferry back to São Vicente.

Day 7 **Cidade Velha**

Take a bus to Cidade Velha (Old Town), a Unesco World Heritage site west of Praia. Check out the ruins of the cathedral, the pillory where enslaved captives were once chained up and walk up the hill to Fortaleza Real de São Filipe for stunning views.

CONTENTS

INTRODUCTION

Rising in a cluster from the stormy Atlantic, the islands which make up the tiny West African nation of Cape Verde are extraordinarily varied. Hop from one to the next and you could be burying your toes in powder-soft sand one day and striding up a country track as steep as a staircase the next. You could be snorkelling with loggerhead turtles and listening to whalesong, or soaking up the impassioned strains of a fiddle and guitar band; sipping caipirinhas in a sophisticated café, or sharing a bowl of maize and beans with a family of farmers; contemplating a lonely hillside with not a soul in sight, or shaking your booty with the rest of the crazy crowd at an all-singing, all-dancing carnival parade.

Natural Beauty

Geographically, the nine inhabited islands are divided into two groups situated around 600km (370 miles) west of Senegal – the Ilhas de Sotavento, or leeward islands, to the south, and the Ilhas de Barlovento, or windward islands, to the north. It's arguably more convenient, however, to think of them as three groups of three: the desert islands of Sal, Boa Vista and Maio to the east, the mountainous islands of Santiago, Fogo and Brava to the southwest, and the mountainous islands of

The cliff-hugging village of Fontainhas on Santo Antão

Inter-island rivalry

Every Cape Verdean will tell you, without hesitation, that theirs is the most beautiful island in the archipelago. The principles of friendly competition are stretched to an extreme in Mindelo, which considers Praia uncultured, unsophisticated and an unworthy capital; Praia, in return, brazenly dismisses the Mindelenses as pedants and snobs.

The stunning dunes of Praia de Chaves on Boa Vista

São Vicente, Santo Antão and São Nicolau to the northwest. Their combined surface area is just over 4,000 sq km (1,500 sq miles).

All the islands are volcanic in origin, but all are very different in age, and this makes their landscapes diverse in the extreme. The oldest islands to the east are weatherworn and flat, while the conspicuously active volcano of Fogo in the southwest is a near-perfect cone. In between are the middle-aged islands, their fires long extinguished but their mountains still strikingly jagged and steep. All have a dry, tropical climate, lying in the direct path of the northeasterly trade winds which once powered transatlantic adventurers to these shores, and now attract windsurfers and kitesurfers in search of the ultimate adrenalin high.

The islands' many kilometres of coastline include rocky shelves containing pools and blowholes; dazzling strands of white, crushed coral; and dramatic black beaches of fine dark lava gravel. Beneath the surface are ancient marine deposits, lava caves and coral reefs patrolled by tropical fish, turtles, dolphins and whales, as well as shipwrecks and their scattered cargo. On land, the landscape is shaped by the availability of water – some areas rely on seasonal downpours, some are watered by condensation or by natural springs, but vast tracts of land receive no water whatsoever from one year to the next. A large proportion of the island terrain is cultivated or grazed to some degree, so a network of protected areas has been created with a view to preserving the islands' endangered and endemic flora and fauna, which include birds, reptiles, spiders, lichens and wild flowers.

Blend of Cultures

Cape Verde has the distinction of being the oldest Creole society in Africa, and one of the most successful African-European communities in the world. Youthful, dynamic and progressive, the population of just over 500,000 is highly educated, its isolation diminishing all the time thanks to the internet and satellite television. Having struggled through periods of severe hardship caused by drought, disease and enforced emigration, Cape Verdeans have great strength of character. Visitors can pick up traces of this in their cultural traditions, such as the heartfelt lyrics of *morna* ballads and the feisty rhythms of *batuko* dances.

Cape Verdeans are almost all of mixed race – part African, part European, but ultimately quite distinct.

A sculpture celebrating Cape Verde's musical heritage

A holiday resort on Sal

Unlike the majority of mainland West Africans, most of the islanders are Catholics who dress in Western style and could be mistaken for Brazilians rather than sub-Saharans. Many include West African slaves among their ancestors, but the violent separation of the slaves from their tribal traditions has meant that connections with specific parts of the mainland have been diluted and lost over time. Instead, most people consider themselves 100 percent Cape Verdean, and the country is characterised by a remarkable atmosphere of ethnic, religious and cultural tolerance. Class discrimination is almost unknown. The one thing Cape Verdeans lack is a full-blown sense of self-determination – many in this nation of emigrants rely on expatriate relatives and connections for income and opportunities. If ever you see an unusually large and well-appointed house in the country, you can be sure that it belongs to somebody who is employed overseas and bringing money home.

The islands' official language is still Portuguese, a legacy of the colonial days, but Cape Verdeans have their own language, Creole (*crioulo* in Portuguese, *kriolu* in the Sotaventos and *kriole* in the Barlaventos), derived from a blend of Portuguese, African languages and English. Creole culture is a matter of fierce national pride. Considered a dialect, Creole spelling and grammar have never been taught in Cape Verdean schools, but there's a growing movement to promote it to the status of official language – as long as all the islanders can agree on which local variant is the most authentic version. If you're travelling widely in Cape Verde, you'll hear Creole spoken all the time, and you may find it easier to learn some than to try to communicate in Portuguese.

Recent Growth

Before 2006, Cape Verde was little known outside Portugal and the only Europeans to visit were windsurfers, Portuguese with long-standing connections and a handful of other in-the-know travellers. In recent years, tourism has grown rapidly, with a boom in resort development, a flurry of interest in real estate and a surge in direct flights. Most of the activity has been concentrated in southwest Sal and on Boa Vista, but there are also large-scale developments in progress on São Vicente and Santiago.

It would be a mistake to come here expecting a slick, Western-style set up. Until 2007, Cape Verde was classed among the 50 least developed countries (LDC) by the United Nations. It is now officially a developing nation and has huge problems to tackle: begging, unsightly litter build-up and poor-quality housing with inadequate sanitation are among the more visible symptoms. However, the government's ongoing commitment to investing in infrastructure and safeguarding the environment bodes well for the future.

Local sentiments

The essence of Cape Verde is summed up in two powerful sentiments: *morabeza*, the warm welcome offered to others, and *sodade*, a nostalgic yearning that expresses itself in the homesickness of the emigrant and the sadness of those left behind.

A BRIEF HISTORY

Formed by a succession of volcanic eruptions caused by the explosion of underwater hotspots between 100,000 and 60 million years ago, the Cape Verde islands were first mapped by seafarers in the 14th and 15th centuries, and named after the westernmost point of the West African mainland, Cap Vert in Senegal, where present-day Dakar is located.

Exploration and Settlement

There's no evidence to suggest that the islands had ever had any permanent residents when they were first claimed on behalf of Prince Henry the Navigator of Portugal between 1460 and 1462. At this point, the Cap Vert peninsula was already an entrepôt for African-European trade, including the buying and selling of slaves, so the islands seemed to be a useful strategic acquisition.

The records of which explorers discovered exactly which islands are rather sketchy – candidates include the Genovese seafarer António da Noli; Diogo Gomes from Portugal, who sailed here in 1445 and whose statue is in Praia; the Venetian Alvise Cadamosto, who first arrived in 1456; and Diogo Afonso from Portugal, who explored the western islands and is honoured by a statue in Mindelo.

Statue of explorer Diogo Gomes in Praia

António da Noli returned in 1462 and founded the settlement of Ribeira Grande at the site of present-day Cidade

The island of São Vicente was discovered in 1462

Velha, bringing in slaves as labourers to grow crops and build houses. The other islands, meanwhile, were used as grazing for livestock which could be sold as ships' supplies.

Among the famous explorers who made a stop at Cape Verde around this time were Vasco da Gama (1497), en route to India; Christopher Columbus (1498), who spent a week visiting Sal, Boa Vista, Santiago and Fogo and remarked on the inappropriateness of the name 'Cabo Verde', as there seemed so little greenery on the islands and Pedro Alvares Cabral (1500), on his voyage of discovery to Brazil.

The Trading Years

Ribeira Grande's early population consisted of Portuguese traders and West African slaves who had been brought in as labourers to grow crops and build houses. Next came various 'undesirables' from Portugal who had been banished by the Catholic state: these included assorted shiploads of

Fortaleza de São Filipe, built in 1587 to protect Ribeira Grande

criminals, Jews and other political or religious dissidents. Many of the settlers went on to have children with slave women, producing the first of many generations of mixed-race Cape Verdeans, the ancestors of the present-day Creole population.

Situated at an ocean crossroads between several lucrative trade routes, running from Europe to India, from West Africa to Spanish Latin America and from Portugal to Brazil, the settlers found themselves perfectly placed to profit from provisioning European galleons with food and water for their long journeys to and from the colonies.

Ribeira Grande also became known as a trading base in its own right, dealing in slaves, salt, hides and *pano* cloth, which was woven from cotton grown on Fogo, and considered extremely valuable. In the 17th century, when Ribeira Grande's slave market was at its busiest, prices charged were considerably higher than on the African mainland, but this was considered money well spent, as the colony's harbour was far safer than anywhere on the Guinea coast. Furthermore, a slave who had made it here in one piece was likely to be healthy and may well have been baptised a Christian; some even spoke a little Portuguese. Most slaves were bound for the Caribbean and Latin America, with the Portuguese crown claiming a percentage of each sale.

News of the colony's growing prosperity spread, and at times when Portugal was the enemy of either England or

France, Ribeira Grande was vulnerable to attack. Francis Drake led a comprehensive attack on the colony in 1585, causing widespread destruction. The construction of a fort, Fortaleza de São Filipe, on the hilltop above the town was not enough to deter further raiders, who continued to strike throughout the 17th century. The most destructive attack of all, mounted in 1712 by a French force led by Jacques Cassard, left the town's cathedral in ruins. Licking their wounds, the islanders fled Ribeira Grande to the more easily defended, fortress-like Platô (Plateau), overlooking the broad harbour of Praia de Santa Maria, now known as Praia da Gambôa. The new town of Praia was declared the official capital in 1770.

Historic Towns and Villages

Cape Verde has a wealth of colonial-era buildings, including fortifications, churches and *sobrados*, the elegant two-storey balconied townhouses favoured by the Portuguese. The remains of the islands' oldest settlement, Ribeira Grande on Santiago, can be explored at Cidade Velha, Cape Verde's principal heritage area, with archaeological sites dating back to 1495, a fort from 1587 (restored, and in good condition), plus cottages and churches from the 16th and 17th centuries.

Vila da Ribeira Brava on São Nicolau also dates from the 17th century, although most of its old buildings are 19th-century. On Boa Vista, you can see the ruins of Sal Rei's offshore fort, completed in 1820, and *sobrados* in various states of repair dating from the remainder of the century; São Filipe on Fogo has many fine buildings of a similar period. Much of Mindelo on São Vicente dates from the mid-19th century, its coaling station heyday, including the Customs House (1860), the parish church (1862) and several merchants' houses. Praia's Platô area was laid out between the 18th and early 20th centuries.

Droughts and Disasters

From the late 18th century until relatively recently, Cape Verde became trapped in a cycle of poverty as it lurched from one devastating drought to the next. By the 1770s, years of overgrazing, which had been commonplace since the 16th century, had ruined much of the terrain, and the colony's population was too large to support itself through several years of failed crops. When famine began to bite, many thousands died; others were abducted as slaves, or tricked into a life of virtual slavery on the Portuguese-run cocoa plantations of São Tomé and Príncipe. Periods of little or no rain recurred at shorter and shorter intervals until by the early 20th century, devastation was hitting roughly once every decade.

There were pockets of good fortune in the midst of this suffering, however. The mid- to late 19th century was a boom time for São Vicente, thanks to the steamship refuelling business established at Mindelo by British importers of Welsh coal. Mindelo's broad harbour is the only one in Cape Verde to enjoy a degree of shelter from the islands' fierce winds all year round, and it was therefore the preferred stopover for vessels crossing the Atlantic between Europe and the Americas, or heading south to southern Africa and Asia. Mindelo prospered up to the end of the Boer War (1899–1902), when British troops refuelled here on the way to and from the Transvaal in South Africa. Soon after, the Portuguese raised local duties and the refuelling business collapsed.

Darwin drops by

Several naturalists came to Cape Verde in the 19th century, including Charles Darwin (1832), on the first voyage of the *Beagle*. Darwin was fascinated by the contrast between the arid and lush regions, and collected many zoological specimens, including the Cape Verde sparrow (*Passer iagoensis*).

OFERECIDO PELA
CÂMARA MUNICIPAL DO PORTO.

Mindelo's railroad, built to transport coal to the seafront

The Struggle for Independence

The horizons of the Cape Verdean population broadened steadily throughout the 19th and 20th centuries through their connections with the US and Lusophone Africa. Many islanders, particularly from Brava and Fogo, went to work on American whaling ships, and ended up settling in New England. Meanwhile the Portuguese colonial governors considered Cape Verdeans the most suitable of all their African subjects for positions of responsibility, and it was common for Cape Verdeans to be offered training for administrative jobs in other colonies.

In the years following World War II, Cape Verdeans who had made it to Europe to study were influenced by young revolutionaries from other African colonies including Angola, Mozambique and Senegal, and an independence movement began to gather momentum. One of its leading lights was the Guinean Marxist politician Amílcar Cabral, who founded

Amílcar Cabral, freedom
fighter and national hero

the PAIGC, the precursor to Cape Verde's present-day ruling party, the PAICV.

The Africans' hopes for a peaceful transfer of power were dashed when it became clear that Portugal's dictator, António de Oliveira Salazar, had no intention of relinquishing the colonies lightly. Lusophone Africa, including Cape Verde, entered a long and bitter armed struggle; very little fighting took place on the islands, however, as African forces focused their attacks on Portuguese military bases on the mainland. An end finally came in 1974 when the Portuguese dictatorship was overthrown, and Portugal set about withdrawing from its colonies as rapidly as possible.

Independent Cape Verde

Independence came on 5 July 1975, bringing one of the other founders of the PAIGC, Aristides Pereira, to power as the country's first president. A coup in Guinea-Bissau five years later prompted Cape Verde to effect a political split from its old ally by forming its own party, the Partido Africano da Independência de Cabo Verde (PAICV). In 1990, Cape Verde abolished its single-party system and became a multiparty unitary republic, governed by national assembly. A new opposition party, the Movimento para a Democracia (MpD), promptly came to power, and ruled for two terms. The PAICV has since been re-elected three times.

Cape Verde Today

In 2007, Cape Verde graduated from Least Developed Country (LDC) to developing country status, as classified by the United Nations. In 2014 it was one of the highest ranking African nations in terms of stability and human development growth. Commerce and services are the country's main earners, with tourism and foreign investment playing an increasingly significant role. With this in mind, the forward-thinking democratic government has been devoting considerable resources to upgrading airports, roads and services, and encouraging and promoting development opportunities. A windfarm constructed on four islands in 2011 supplies around 30 percent of the country's electricity.

Amílcar Cabral

Born to Cape Verdean parents in Portuguese Guinea (present-day Guinea-Bissau) in 1924 and educated in Lisbon, Amílcar Cabral became one of the driving forces behind the Lusophone African nationalist movement which arose in the 1950s. Cabral, tragically, did not live to see independence: he was assassinated by a political rival in January 1973.

Cabral, who believed in a unified Cape Verde and Guinea-Bissau, founded the PAIGC (the African Party for the Independence of Guinea Bissau and Cape Verde) to represent both nations' desire for a peaceful transition to independence. Guinea-Bissau was severely impoverished and had much to gain from the alliance.

When peaceful negotiations with the Portuguese failed, the PAIGC turned to guerrilla warfare, strikes and finally a declaration of war, issued by Cabral in 1963. Using arms supplied by the USSR, China and Cuba, their forces started wiping out Portuguese military targets in Guinea-Bissau.

Cabral is still regarded as a hero in Cape Verde. There's a large statue of him near the government buildings in Praia, Sal airport is named after him, and almost every town has a major street bearing his name.

In recent years, Cape Verde has enjoyed special partnership status with the EU and sought to strengthen ties with the US. In 2013 the Cape Verdean government announced that the name "The Republic of Cabo Verde," Portuguese in origin, would be used for all official purposes and should no longer be translated into other languages.

Realising that Cape Verde is capable of offering its visitors more than just tropical sunshine and beaches, the authorities have also begun beautifying the country's cultural assets – museums, colonial ruins and historic facades. The Hotel and Tourism School for Cape Verde in Praia helps islanders to become fully multilingual and get to grips with European tourists' priorities and foibles. Meanwhile, environmentalists are monitoring the situation carefully, mindful that unchecked development could cause irrevocable damage to fragile flora and wildlife habitats.

A fisherman takes a break

Historical Landmarks

1460 Portuguese claim the islands as their first West African settlement.
1462 The first settlers arrive at António da Noli's camp at Ribeira Grande on Santiago.
1480s–1540s Settlers arrive on Fogo, Brava, Santo Antão and São Nicolau, and Cape Verde is declared a Portuguese colony.
1585 Francis Drake and a thousand-strong force attack all of the settlements on Santiago.
1680 Fogo erupts with great violence.
1712 Jacques Cassard leads French pirates in an attack on Ribeira Grande.
1770 Praia becomes the new capital.
1772 Severe drought hits, and fatal famines recur many times over the following century.
1838 Mindelo's steamship refuelling business takes off.
1902 The islands are hit by the first of another series of droughts which claim many lives in the 20th century.
1956 Amílcar Cabral and other political activists create the PAIGC and launch the Guinea-Bissau and Cape Verde independence movement.
1960 The PAIGC begins an armed rebellion that develops into a war between Portuguese Guinea and Portugal.
1975 On 5 July, Cape Verde receives independence from Portugal and Aristides Pereira becomes the first president.
1980 Cape Verde separates politically from Guinea-Bissau with the foundation of the PAICV.
1991 Cape Verde's first multi-party elections are won by the MpD.
1995 Fogo erupts.
2008 Cape Verde joins the World Trade Organisation.
2011 The PAICV wins parliamentary elections for the third time in a row; Jorge Carlos Fonseca becomes president.
2011 Two days of national mourning are declared following the death of *morna* singer Cesária Évora.
2014 Fogo residents are evacuated following a powerful eruption of the Pico do Fogo volcano, one of the strongest ever recorded on the island.

WHERE TO GO

While there's much to be gained from exploring just one or two Cape Verdean islands in depth, the country is so fascinatingly diverse that island-hopping tours can be extremely rewarding. With nine very different inhabited islands to choose from, it's possible to plan a varied itinerary to suit one's specific interests. With careful planning, you could easily take in Sal or Boa Vista plus two or three more islands in a week, or up to four or five islands in a fortnight, hopping from one to the next by internal flight or inter-island ferry.

WHICH ISLANDS?

Here is a brief guide to what you'll find on each island, followed by more detailed coverage of sights and attractions throughout the archipelago.

Sal

The island that's most geared towards tourism, with direct access from the UK and a good variety of hotels, restaurants and watersports facilities in its developing southern resort, Santa Maria.

Good for: watersports, beach hotels, live music, desert landscapes, turtles.

Look elsewhere for: mountains, hiking, authentic charm.

Boa Vista

Like Sal, a desert island with direct access from the UK, but with fewer hotels and restaurants, less of a resort scene and more attractive scenery, including beautiful dunes.

Cidade Velha

Good for: watersports, beach hotels, dunes and desert landscapes, turtles.
Look elsewhere for: mountains, hiking, urban vibe.

Maio

Not yet ready for mainstream tourism, a desert island with simple traditional villages, exposed beaches and a lot of empty space.
Good for: desert landscapes, turtles, peace and quiet.
Look elsewhere for: mountains, hiking, urban vibe, gastronomy.

Santiago

The island with the biggest city (Praia) and the most varied scenery, with historic ruins, green landscapes and interesting villages to explore.
Good for: authentic urban vibe, live music, folk culture,

Catch of the day

mountains, hiking, bird-watching.
Look elsewhere for: desert landscapes.

Fogo
The only island that's a live volcano, with a peak to climb and dramatic lava fields to admire, plus a charming capital (São Filipe) and a thriving coffee- and wine-making tradition.
Good for: unique volcanic landscapes, hiking, bird-watching, folk culture, authentic charm.
Look elsewhere for: beach hotels, watersports, desert.

Brava
Reached by ferry, an extremely pretty, untouristy and friendly little island which inspires musicians, writers and artists.
Good for: mountains, hiking, bird-watching, authentic charm, peace and quiet.
Look elsewhere for: beach hotels, watersports, swimming pools, desert.

São Vicente
The island with the most diverting and cosmopolitan town (Mindelo), home to many famous Cape Verdean musicians, and easy access to Santo Antão by ferry.
Good for: authentic urban vibe, café society, live music, desert landscapes.
Look elsewhere for: hiking, watersports.

Santo Antão
Reached by ferry, a dramatically beautiful island with wonderful green vistas and the best variety of hiking routes in Cape Verde.
Good for: mountains, lush scenery, hiking, bird-watching, authentic charm, peace and quiet.
Look elsewhere for: watersports, urban vibe.

São Nicolau

A very quiet and untouristy island with pretty towns, highly varied scenery and very friendly people.

Good for: mountains, hiking, bird-watching, authentic charm, peace and quiet.

Look elsewhere for: beach hotels, watersports, swimming pools, sand dunes, urban vibe.

SAL

Sal's greatest asset, its long and lovely coastline, looks ravishing from the air. Fringed by crystal clear water and pale, sandy beaches, the south is particularly appealing.

First impressions of the interior from ground level can be less favourable, however, particularly for those unlucky enough to arrive on a grey day. Much of the island consists of barren expanses of windy, rock-strewn desert, with tumble-down cement-block shacks dotted here and there, and little vegetation apart from a few stunted acacia trees. To the north loom the dark remains of ancient volcanoes; otherwise, the landscape is extremely flat. The approach to Santa Maria, the main resort, is unprepossessing, with cranes bristling all along the coastal zone where rows of apartment blocks are taking shape.

Despite these initial disappointments, many visitors find the island grows on them. Santa Maria has a relaxed, raffish charm, and its beaches offer perfect conditions for watersports.

Santa Maria

First settled in 1830, **Santa Maria**, at Sal's southern tip, was the island's first capital and a major salt production centre. When the island government moved to Espargos in 1981, to be closer to the airport, Santa Maria gradually declined, until tourism turned its fortunes around.

In recent years Santa Maria has mushroomed from an impoverished village into a full-blown resort, ribboning along the coast; it is now the biggest town on the island. There are plans for an almost unbroken band of development from the heart of the old village, where islanders used to scratch a living from fishing, all the way along to Murdeira Bay. Thus far, most of the hotels and apartments that have been built are aimed at the middle market but new luxury resorts are emerging.

For now, Santa Maria remains at a transitional stage, as it learns how best to cater for a steady stream of European holidaymakers, and its population absorbs a growing contingent of construction and tourism workers from other islands and from the West African mainland. Santa Maria is far more multicultural than anywhere else in Cape Verde: it has a sizeable community of European expats and is the only town where traditional West African dress is commonplace,

Praia de Santa Maria is popular with windsurfers

thanks to the influx of Mauritanians, Senegalese, Gambians and Guinea-Bissauans.

Architecturally, much of the old character of the village has already been lost as single-storey fishermen's cottages have been torn down to make room for unremarkable new apartment buildings. But despite the developers' best attempts to rip the heart out of Santa Maria, the welcoming spirit of the local population, buoyed up by new opportunities, survives intact.

The village is centred on a wide, sandy bay with a very spacious beach, **Praia de Santa Maria**. Its pale sand and sparkling turquoise and sapphire sea is certainly impressive, but sunbathers and swimmers should bear in mind that there's no natural shade, and the wind and undertow can be fierce, particularly in winter. Edging the beach is a promenade which connects the village with the string of hotels along the western edge of the bay and beyond.

Curio Hunting

Impossible to avoid in Santa Maria are the great many stall-like shops selling carvings, bead necklaces, batiks and djembé drums which, though African in style, have no cultural connection with Cape Verde – you may even see elephants and giraffes among the designs. Most of these souvenirs are imported from the West African mainland, but some are made in the Far East.

Whether or not you're interested, it's worth being wise to the hard-sell techniques of the vendors. Some hire touts – typically from mainland West Africa, rather than from Cape Verde – to lure you in with free gifts and promises. There's no need to feel pressured: a friendly but firm 'no thank you' will invariably result in them moving off in search of a more fruitful target. If you do decide to buy, haggle hard, and don't be too concerned if the vendor shows grave offence – this is usually part of the game. No vendor will sell you something at a discount he can't afford.

Santa Maria has few sights in the conventional sense. The natural focus of village life is still the **Pontão** (jetty) at which fishermen unload their catch. With each new arrival, the area buzzes with activity. The fish are promptly gutted and cleaned then loaded onto wheelbarrows to be rushed into town and dispensed to hotel and restaurant kitchens. At other times,

Trinkets on sale in Santa Maria

local teenagers amuse themselves by diving off the end of the jetty into the transparent water, where colourfully painted boats bob about. At the foot of the jetty is the **White House**, a former headquarters of the local salt trade, which is now home to a café and gift shop.

Inland from the jetty is a grid of streets in which the rather plain parish church, **Igreja de Nossa Senhora das Dores** (Our Lady of Sorrows), presides over rows of laidback boutiques, bars and fish restaurants, some of them occupying a few of the remaining single-storey cottages. The village square, **Praça de Marcelo Leitão**, features a replica of the type of timber windmill that was used as a water pump in Sal's salt flats in the early 18th century.

After eating, drinking and simple relaxation, shopping is the preferred activity in town. One of the best places for hand-crafted souvenirs is **Oficina de Arte** on Rua 1 de Junho, near Café Criolo: adjoining the shop is a workshop where artisans create stylish ceramic bottles and pots. For quality African souvenirs at fixed prices, it's worth checking out the **Akuaba** gallery shop on the street leading to the jetty: the carvings, textiles, bags, jewellery and homewares here are expensive, but beautifully chosen.

The disused salt works at Pedra de Lume

Sal is regarded as one of the five best locations for windsurfing in the world. Watersports stations catering for windsurfers, kiteboarders, surfers and scuba-divers are dotted along the beach in Santa Maria. The coolest quarter for windsurfers and surfers to hang out is around **Praia de António Sousa** at the affluent east end of town, but the gnarliest conditions are to be found out of town along the southwest coast, at **Ponta Preta**. Kitesurfers, meanwhile, head out to **Serra Negra** (sometimes called Kite Beach or Shark Bay) on the southeast coast.

Other popular activities in Santa Maria include taking an underwater tour in *Neptunus*, a bright yellow semi-submersible; joy-riding on a banana boat; going catamaran cruising, waterskiing, snorkelling or fishing; or heading into the desert by quad bike. Hotel staff and holiday reps can fix any of these up, and can also arrange guided day-trips around Sal or to other islands.

Exploring Sal

A tarmac road runs from Santa Maria to the airport and the capital, Espargos, then east to the old salt-production village of Pedra de Lume and west to the port town of Palmeira. It's possible to explore the remainder of the island, such as the west coast and the rugged northern wilderness, in a 4x4 or by mountain bike or quad.

On the coast slightly northwest of Santa Maria is **Ponta Preta**, Cape Verde's most famous windsurfing location, with a sandy beach leading to a rocky point. Here, the year-round trade winds draw champions. Inland from here, a few remnants of old Sal remain, such as the walled **cemetery** just north of town, the chapel of **Nossa Senhora de Fatima** perched beside the main road, and the old *poço*, or waterhole. North of Ponta Preta, at the southern tip of Murdeira Bay, a protected area, is **Calheta Funda**, a bay that's pleasant for swimming.

   Espargos, near the centre of the island, huddles round a low hill bristling with telecom masts. Although not a particularly attractive town, it has a more authentic atmosphere than Santa Maria – its shady main square, low-key bars and laidback street life have a great deal in common with other small towns in the archipelago, and it can be a good place to try some Creole cooking, such as *sopa de mão de vaca* (cow's foot soup), or catch some genuine traditional music. The **Escola Municipal de Arte Tututa**, offers music, dance and theatre tuition aimed at versing

The Salt Islands

From the mid-16th to the mid-20th century, sea salt – crucial for prolonging the life of fresh food in the absence of refrigeration – was Cape Verde's most valuable commodity. Production took place on Sal, Boa Vista and Maio, where the flat coastal terrain contained natural salt pans. Initially, slaves were forced to do the back-breaking work of shovelling the salt into sacks and loading it onto donkeys for transportation to the ports. Much of Cape Verde's output ended up in the Americas.

   However, a shift in the global market caused this industry to decline in the 20th century, dying out completely in the 1980s. Today, only a few artisans harvest the salt from the remaining pans, scraping the crystals into pyramids and leaving them to dry. It's possible to buy little bags of hand-harvested salt in gift shops.

Saltwater spa

Today, the Salinas at Pedra de Lume operate as a rudimentary spa – for a small charge, visitors can bathe in the salty water, which is considered highly therapeutic, or enjoy a relaxing massage. The salt content of the pools is higher than that of the Dead Sea, making floating effortless.

young people in traditional culture, and possibly preparing them for a career in entertainment.

The **Salinas** (salt works) at the east coast village of **Pedra de Lume** are a Cape Verdean National Heritage Site and one of the island's most interesting features. Here, salt forms naturally on the floor of an extinct volcanic crater which lies close enough to the sea to flood with sea water by way of channels. These salt deposits have been exploited commercially since 1804 and were initially manned by slaves, who undertook the arduous task of tunnelling through the crater wall so that salt could be easily carried out from the crater floor and down to the village harbour. Productivity rocketed in the early 20th century when a French-Senegalese firm built a 1,100-metre (3,600ft) cableway to enable sacks to be transported out at a rate of 25 tonnes per hour. Large-scale operations closed down in the late 1980s, but the rather ghostly remains of the cableway are still standing.

On the island's west coast is **Palmeira**, site of Sal's docks, due to be upgraded, its power station, which may be supplemented by wind turbines in due course, and its main desalination plant. From here, a track leads north along the coast to the **Buracona** lava rock pools and the **Olho Azul** (Blue Eye), a pool which appears to glow with eerie blue light when the sun shines at a certain angle. The rest of the north consists of rugged, weather-worn *ribeiras*, lashed by crashing waves and explored only by adventurous off-roaders.

BOA VISTA

Boa Vista, the island immediately south of Sal, is a desert island of soft, shifting dunes, rocky plains and eroded volcanoes, so sparsely populated that it's possible to walk for miles without seeing a soul. Like Sal, it has gloriously wide, open beaches on its south and west coasts, and these have attracted developers. Boa Vista already has several large resort-style hotels and an international airport and is slowly becoming as popular with holidaymakers as Sal.

The salty winds that tear across the island for most of the year apply a coating of sand to every stationary object. Derelict buildings, abandoned when hard-up farmers and fishermen leave in search of a better living, soon become half-engulfed, and such vegetation as there is – a few palm oases, some lowly acacias and succulents – have a permanently forlorn, dusty look. To some, the desert scenery, stretched out under huge skies, is very beautiful; to others, it's unsettlingly barren.

Windsurfing, kitesurfing, scuba-diving and off-roading are all popular here. None are quite as developed as on Sal, though this is likely to change as visitor numbers continue to climb. Unfortunately, however, the

Bathing in the salt water
pools at Pedra de Lume

Boa Vista's barren interior is dotted with extinct volcanoes

growth in tourism brings environmental concerns: litter is a problem on the island, and beach development is damaging delicate wildlife habitats, with serious consequences for endangered species such as the loggerhead turtles which nest here in the summer.

Sal Rei

Like the other flat islands of eastern Cape Verde, Boa Vista was discovered by Portuguese seafarers in May 1460, and came to be used as grazing land for livestock, to the detriment of its desert-adapted vegetation. Later, English adventurers spotted its potential as a place to harvest sea salt. As production took off, the island inevitably began to attract unwanted attention from pirates; the solution was to build the Fortaleza de Duque de Braganza on the Ilhéu de Sal Rei, a flat islet just off the islet's northwest coast. This fort was completed in the 1820s; efficiently defended, the stage was now set for the mainland settlement of **Sal Rei** to become a prosperous salt-industry town. Such was its success that later in the 19th century there was a movement to make it the capital of Cape Verde.

In its glory days, Sal Rei was a far grander settlement than Santa Maria. Echoes of the past remain in its spacious main square, **Largo de Santa Isabel**, and imposing parish church, the **Igreja de Santa Isabel**. Between the square and the harbour are cobbled streets lined with relatively large buildings, including a few *sobrados* – elegant, balconied townhouses built by the Portuguese. Out on the uninhabited **Ilhéu de Sal Rei** are the remains of the fort; if you ask a fisherman to ferry you across, you'll find some of its cannons are intact.

When the salt industry declined, Sal Rei hit the buffers, and it still has a rather unloved appearance. Its popularity with European developers, particularly Italians, has given it a boost, and there are building projects in progress all over town. The *praça* has also been spruced up, with a new children's playground, banks and other businesses. This renewed prosperity has not been evenly shared, however, and many townspeople, including the women washing clothes in the public sinks near the beach, or selling fish from buckets, are poor.

Stretching south from Sal Rei is a long, beautiful beach, **Praia do Estoril**, that's superb for strolling. Colourful fishing boats and a few yachts hug the harbour, while, further out in Estoril Bay, windsurfers and kitesurfers scud along. Humpback whales may occasionally be seen breaching here in the winter months. Glimmering in the distance like a fantastical desert palace

Igreja de Santa Isabel

is the Riu Karamboa, an all-inclusive resort; beyond this are the gorgeous dunes of Praia de Chaves.

Exploring Boa Vista

It's easy for confident 4x4 drivers, with good experience of sandy conditions, to cover most of the island in a single day. Touring by mountain bike can also be very rewarding as long as you prepare for the dehydrating effects of the sun and wind.

North of Sal Rei, **Praia da Cruz** is edged with a growing number of new buildings. On the north coast is the **Baía de Boa Esperança**, where the shattered, rusting remains of the *Cabo Santa Maria*, a Spanish cargo ship, lie just offshore, scoured by the waves. It was beached in September 1968 on its return journey from Brazil and Argentina, unevenly loaded with a cargo of cars, machinery and clothing, intended as gifts from General Franco to his supporters. It wasn't the first ship to meet an untimely end here: the beach used to be called Praia da Atalanta after a Scandinavian three-masted sailing ship which ran aground on Christmas Eve, 1920.

The main road south out of Sal Rei is shadowed by an older route, the **Via Pitoresca**, which was probably much more picturesque before drought ravaged its palm trees. After around 3km (2 miles), the old road rejoins the main road leading to the airport and the small town of **Rabil**, home to many of the island's construction, farming and tourism workers. On Rabil's southern edge is a terracotta workshop, the **Escola de Olaria**, where craftsmen

Making tracks in the Deserto de Viana

Relaxing on beautiful Praia de Chaves

make moulded pots, tiles and souvenir turtles. Its opening hours are irregular, so if it's closed, it's worth asking around nearby for someone to let you in.

Just east of Rabil are some of Boa Vista's most beautiful dunes, the gorgeously soft, bone-white **Deserto de Viana**. Geologists believe that the eruptions that resulted in the formation of Boa Vista brought the remains of ancient marine fossils to the surface, making the fine sand of the Viana Desert the oldest in the archipelago.

Praia de Chaves, west of Rabil and south of Sal Rei, is a stunning beach of pale sand with the chimney of an old brickworks nestled among its luscious dunes. There are several hotels here, but the sand is so wide and long that the sense of open space is barely compromised. The turquoise sea can be rather wild, however, and is often unsafe for swimming.

South of Rabil is **Povoação Velha**, Boa Vista's first settlement; sleepy in the extreme, this half-derelict village has

Friendly faces in João Galego village

seen little activity since the island's focus moved to Sal Rei and Rabil 200 years ago. The remainder of the south of the island is crisscrossed by a few rough tracks. To the southwest is the breathtakingly long and very exposed **Praia de Santa Mónica**. This beautiful beach feels truly wild and isolated, backed only by rough heathland, but there are plans afoot to build another giant tourist resort here.

Inland from Rabil, a cobbled road crosses the **Campo da Serra**, a multi-hued desert landscape of ginger, burnt umber and beige, scattered with rocks and low vegetation. Goats, cattle and donkeys may sometimes be seen wandering the plain, even though there appears to be next to nothing for them to graze on. Rising above the uniform horizon to the south and east are the island's highest peaks, including **Monte Estância** and **Santo António**. None of these extinct volcanoes is higher than 400 metres (1,300ft), but their flat surroundings make them seem considerably higher.

On the east side of the plain, the landscape becomes a little greener, and the road passes through three hamlets, collectively called **Norte**. The first, **João Galego**, is little more than a single street with a community centre marked by paintings of political hero Amílcar Cabral, and a small square. This village is considered a good place to buy locally produced goat's cheese. The next, **Fundo das Figueiras**, is the largest and prettiest of the three, its handful of shady streets lined with single-storey houses. Hibiscus bushes, swathes of bougainvillea, brightly painted walls and contrasting shutters all add splashes of colour to the scene. The village church, **Igreja de São João Baptista**, is refreshingly austere, with an Arts and Crafts-style wooden altar table, altar seats and pulpit. The third village, **Cabeço das Tarafes**, is a small cluster of houses and a bar.

Further south of here is another isolated bay, **Praia de Ervatão**. A group of naturalists have been monitoring the effects of tourism and poaching on the loggerhead turtles which clamber up the sand to lay their eggs here.

MAIO

Maio feels different to its busier neighbours, Sal and Boa Vista. While its desert scenery is similar and its pale, sandy beaches are just as wild and open, the developers have practically passed it by. Instead of rows of new apartments and villas, Maio has villages of single-storey fishermen's cottages, interspersed with sizeable expanses of sparsely vegetated scrubland,

Turtle protection

Cape Verde is the best place in the Atlantic to see loggerhead turtles, which nest on its beaches in summer. Tragically, however, these endangered turtles are severely threatened by poachers, encroaching development, and thoughtless destruction of nests by vehicles and quad bikes. To learn more, contact SOS Tartarugas (www.turtlesos. org) or the Turtle Foundation (www.turtle-foundation.org).

Fishing boats on the beach,
Vila do Maio

nibbled by a few hardy goats and donkeys. The only new buildings that exist are low-rise and modest in extent.

This is the closest island to Praia – the flight is over in a flash – so in theory it's a more obvious beach retreat for city-dwellers than Tarrafal in northern Santiago. However, a catalogue of inter-island transport problems combined with a lack of tourist infrastructure has restricted the flow of visitors to a trickle. When you land at the decidedly low-tech aerodrome, you may find that you are the only non-natives to arrive that day.

For the first couple of centuries after its discovery in May 1460, the Portuguese used Maio as grazing for livestock – a damaging practice from which the delicate dunelands have never recovered. In the late 16th century, the British established a basic settlement on the site of present-day Vila do Maio. This post, which came to be known as Porto Inglês, was used for provisioning galleons and preparing salt for export. At the peak of the trade, Maio was producing 11,000 tonnes of salt per year, and as a result it became a target for buccaneers. Infamous characters including Blackbeard, William Dampier, Francis Drake and Henry Morgan struck from time to time, sometimes setting up camps on the island's more sheltered coves: archaeologists have unearthed buckles, pipes, broken bottles and other oddments they left behind.

Today, Maio's attractions are subtle – its villages, though desperately poor and isolated, are refreshingly unspoilt by tourism, and there's an austere beauty to its silent, arid landscapes.

Vila do Maio

Quiet and practically traffic-free, **Vila do Maio** is more of a village than a town. Arranged behind a beach of dazzlingly pale sand, it has a great many colonial-era buildings which could be very pretty if restored. For now, however, there's a rather stagnant atmosphere to the place. The poverty of the town is further evidenced by the fact that there's practically nothing to buy in the market and some streets and parts of the beach are filthy, as many homes have inadequate sanitation.

The town's most dominant landmark is its impressive church, the **Igreja Matriz de Nossa Senhora da Luz** (Our Lady of Light), built in 1812, uphill from the harbour. For a

Mysteries of the Deep

The treacherous waters surrounding Maio and Boa Vista hide secrets that are arguably more interesting than anything to be found on the surface. Dangerous currents and gusts, hidden reefs and geological conditions which play havoc with traditional navigational equipment have sunk many a ship, often with great loss of life. There are also rumours of impoverished islanders deliberately luring ships to their doom with lights, in order to plunder their cargo.

Wrecks dating back to the 16th century are plentiful – as are tales of buried treasure, pieces of eight and pirate gold, particularly on Maio. Many of the wrecks have never been investigated in detail, but a few have been painstakingly studied by marine archaeologists; a selection of their most fascinating finds, from ivory tusks to manicure sets and bottles of port, are on display at the Archaeology Museum in Praia (see page 51).

A local character, Calheta

parish church, it has a rather grand interior, with a high blue ceiling and an imposing altar. The church and its shady square are the focus of proceedings every 3 May, the feast of Santa Cruz, when a cross is paraded before town as a prelude to a celebratory mass and a feast of chicken soup, stewed goat, ground maize, *grogue* and wine.

The original name for Vila do Maio, Porto Inglês, is still sometimes used, and the **Fortaleza de São José**, the stocky fort which once defended the settlement against marauding pirates, has been restored, close to the harbour steps. You can also see the remains of the vast *salinas* (salt works) along the coast to the north: they're no longer in large-scale commercial operation, but the flats gather plenty of salt.

Exploring Maio

Circumnavigating Maio by vehicle or mountain bike is straightforward: a road loops around the entire island. Most of it is tarmac, but a four-wheel-drive is essential for any in-depth exploration. The west coast is generally sandy, fringed by long, windblown beaches, while the east coast is punctuated by rocky coves. The long-extinct volcano of **Monte Penoso**, which at 436 metres (1,430ft) is Maio's highest peak, dominates the horizon; the interior is otherwise rather featureless apart from a plantation of low acacia trees 10km (6 miles) north of Vila do Maio, rather optimistically termed the **Zona**

Forestal, where charcoal is produced and bagged up for export to the other islands.

Spaced out along the road are several simple hamlets, the prettiest of which is the village of **Calheta**, on the southern edge of the 'forest zone'. It's a relatively upbeat little place with jaunty rows of brightly painted single-storey cottages. Here, fishermen haul their catch of tuna, grouper and lobster onto the beach, or play *oril* (see page 89) in the shade.

North of here are some of Maio's most attractive beaches. They're wild, undeveloped and rather inaccessible, which is good news for the turtles which nest here in July and August. They're also unsafe for swimming, even when the sea is calm. Among the best are **Praia de Santana**, a wide, northwest-facing bay backed by sand dunes and salt flats, and **Praia Real**, facing north.

Nation of Builders

The fringes of almost every Cape Verdean town are marked (scarred, some might say) by unfinished cement-block houses in ugly shades of grey. Nowhere is this more evident than on the affluent and fast-developing island of Santiago.

Some of these buildings are owned by people who are ambitious enough to want to make improvements, but can only afford a little at a time; as such, you could consider them a sign of progress. Many belong to emigrants who come back to their home island every so often to do as much work as their savings allow. Since they're not usually planning to live here permanently until they retire, they're in no hurry to finish the construction, let alone render and paint the walls.

Paradoxically, however, Cape Verdeans are keen decorators. Once their houses are finally complete, they often top them off with a jaunty paint job in contrasting shades of yellow, blue, pink and green.

In the south of the island, there are a few attempts at cultivation, and, near the hamlet of **Ribeira Dom João**, another attractive beach with turquoise sea breaking onto pale sand.

SANTIAGO

As the seat of government and the island with the longest history of human settlement, Santiago has an air of importance which sets it apart from the rest of the archipelago. It is the largest island, at around 55km (34 miles) long and 990 sq km (382 sq miles) in area, and it has by far the highest number of inhabitants: around 272,000, or approximately three-quarters of the entire Cape Verdean population. It's no wonder, then, that some islanders use the names Santiago and Cabo Verde interchangeably. Furthermore, Santiagoenses often call the other islands,

Praia, Cape Verde's capital city

rather dismissively, *As Ilhas* ('The Islands'), and consider their inhabitants thoroughly provincial.

Over a third of the population of Santiago live in the urban sprawl of Praia, the capital, which hugs the island's southernmost bay. Outside the city, there's a remarkable variety of scenery, from sandy beaches to hidden villages and craggy mountainsides draped in lush greenery.

The Monumento ao Emigrante

Praia

While the city of **Praia** doesn't have enough conventional sights to detain visitors for more than a day or two, it is a purposeful city which offers an interesting snapshot of a side of Cape Verde that many tourists miss. With its modern access roads, 19th-century European-style centre, African-style markets, Chinese imports and dynamic, mixed-race population, Praia encapsulates the driving spirit of this post-colonial nation.

Praia's international airport is marked by another powerful emblem of contemporary Cape Verde – the **Monumento ao Emigrante** (Monument to the Emigrant) by Carlos Hamelberg, dedicated to the Cape Verdean diaspora. Created in response to a quote in Creole from Eugénio Tavares, '*Si ka badu, ka ta biradu*' – if you don't leave, you won't return – it's a sail-like abstract mounted on a base covered in rippling blue tiles.

The journey into Praia from the airport is swift. The city centre is divided into three main districts. The **Platô**, a narrow grid of colonial buildings, is concentrated on a plateau of rock

The old Câmara Municipal on Praça Alexandre Albuquerque

overlooking the bay. At its foot is **Chã d'Areia** (literally, sandy plain), an administrative and business district which is home to the Museu de Arqueologia and is fringed by a large, black beach, **Praia da Gambôa**, site of Santiago's biggest annual music festival. The low cliffs on the southwest side of the bay are topped by the city's diplomatic quarter, **Prainha**, where the more upmarket hotels are situated. The surrounding hill-sides are covered by mushrooming residential districts.

Up on the Platô, the city's main square, **Praça de Alexandre Albuquerque**, is pleasantly leafy, with a bandstand, a fountain and busts of two figures who helped shape Lusophone Africa in the 19th century, the eponymous Caetano Alexandre d'Almeida e Albuquerque and Serpa Pinto. There are usually a few shoeshine and snack stalls set up on the Portuguese-style black-and-white cobbled pavements. It's a place where old meets new: you may hear the clatter of beads from *oril*-players relaxing under the trees, but you'll also see knots of laptop users peering at their screens. On the east side of the square is Santiago's cathedral, the **Igreja de Nossa Senhora da Graça** (Church of Our Lady of Grace), which was built in 1902 and has a lofty, wedding-cake-white interior with a grand high altar. On the other side is the **Palácio da Cultura**, which occasionally hosts exhibitions and events, and has a permanent display of work by Cape Verdean artists on its main staircase. To the south is the classical facade of the old **Câmara Municipal** (town hall). Behind this is the **Palácio da República** (presidential palace), which was formerly the colonial governor's residence. Gazing out to sea here is a large **statue of Diogo Gomes**, one of the first European explorers to record the existence of the island.

The surrounding streets are mostly narrow and full of animation and noise. The main produce market, **Mercado do Platô**, north of the square, is a bustling mêlée of buyers and sellers. Seasonal fruit and vegetables and stacked in colourful heaps: depending on the time of year, you may see sweet potatoes, squashes, plump tomatoes, knobbly cabbages, tamarind pods, bananas, mangoes, bunches of dewy coriander, strings of garlic and well-stuffed sacks of beans. In the corners are cool rooms where meat hangs on hooks and fresh groupers, snappers and eels gape from stainless-steel slabs.

Stallholder at the Mercado do Platô

A couple of blocks northeast of the market is a smaller square, **Pracinha da Escola Grande**, with a pleasant café, the best CD shop in town, and the offices of Cape Verde's public university.

Further northwest again on Avenida 5 de Julho is the **Museu Etnográfico da Praia** (Ethnographic Museum; Mon–Fri 9.30am–noon, 2.30–5.30pm; labels mostly in Portuguese), in an elegantly restored 19th-century *sobrado* with high ceilings and polished floors. Well worth a brief visit, the museum displays a collection of man-made objects, mostly from villages in Santiago, which collectively serve to illustrate the islanders' struggle to survive in a hostile rural environment.

Ceramic pot in the Museu Etnográfico da Praia

In the airy upstairs gallery is a particularly fine example of *pano* weaving, which has been practised in Cape Verde since the 17th century, when cotton was cultivated on Fogo. Among the other items are ceramic pots, reminders of a way of life before electrical refrigeration; tools used to pound cereals into flour; and gourds used to carry handmade butter and goat's cheese, a useful source of nutrients to supplement a diet based on fish. There are also beautifully woven baskets, symbolic of social exchange: when visiting another family, it was customary to take a basket full of food, and for the hosts to reciprocate by refilling the basket on their guests' departure, or to retain the basket as a token to show that they owe a return visit.

Downstairs are a few musical instruments, including a *cavaquinho* and a *viola de dez cordas* (10-string guitar), along with some items collected from a farmhouse, such as a bathtub made from a hollowed-out section of a tree trunk and some sandals made from rough leather and rope.

One block back from the museum, on Avenida Amílcar Cabral, is the **Quintal da Música**, Praia's atmospheric live music venue, its walls plastered with photos of Cape Verdean musical greats. It hosts live bands nightly except Sundays. From here, it's a short walk downhill to the **Mercado de Sucupira** (Sucupira Market), a crowded, rambling collection of stalls that feels more West African than any other market in the country.

Further south in Chã d'Areia, near Cabo Verde Telecom, is the **Museu de Arqueologia** (Archaeology Museum; Mon–Fri 9am–noon and 2–6pm), with its small but fascinating permanent exhibition of shipwreck salvage. Most of the items on display were recovered from English galleons which sank in storms off Cape Verde in the 18th and early 19th centuries. Among them is a huge ivory tusk from *the Princess Louisa*, an East India Company vessel which was travelling from London

Pano Cloth

Traditional handwoven cloth has great symbolic, historic and cultural value to the islanders. Typically made out of six long cotton strips sewn together, the weaving is worked in distinctive patterns using just two colours, often black or indigo and white. The more complex the design, the more costly the cloth: variations include *pano chã* (*panú txan* in Creole), with simple stripes; *pano bicho* (*panú bitxu*), with motifs, sometimes in animal shapes; and *pano de obra* (*panú d'obra*), with complex tile-like patterns.

Women used to wear *panos* as wraps, tied around the waist; sometimes they would use them to carry small objects, or to bind their babies to their backs. These days, *panos* are heirlooms and it's relatively rare to see them being worn, but there are examples of looms and finished articles on display in the ethnographic museums in Praia, São Filipe and Mindelo, and you can watch weavers in action at the artisans' centre at São Domingos on Santiago.

In the Museu de Arqueologia

to Persia in 1743 with 820 such tusks on board. There's also a brass plate from the trunk of a Miss Dixon who was sailing to Madras on the *Lady Burgess* with her mother on 1806: the ship struck a reef between Boa Vista and Maio in the middle of the night, and half the crew lost their lives. Happily, the Dixons survived, although their luggage, presumably, did not.

Other striking finds include a gold crucifix inlaid with emeralds and diamonds; hauls of gleaming coins; and a rare and extremely valuable silver-plated mariner's astrolabe (the piece on show is a replica of the original).

Earlier items, found in the waters near Cidade Velha, illuminate the islands' part in the triangle of trade: there are bronze manillas and clay pipes, which served as currency to buy West African slaves, and crucifixes, used by Portuguese slave traffickers intent on converting Africans to Catholicism, a practice by which they justified their capture.

Cidade Velha

Cape Verde's oldest settlement, Ribeira Grande, was founded in 1462 by the Genoese explorer António da Noli, one of several seafarers hired by Prince Henry the Navigator to further Portugal's trading interests. His camp took its name from its deep, fertile riverbed, opening onto a harbour which provided safe anchorage for most of the year.

The present-day village of **Cidade Velha** (Old City) on the southwest coast of the island, west of Praia, stands on the site of Ribeira Grande, and concerted restoration and documentation works have made its fort, churches and ruined cathedral accessible to visitors. In 2009 the assemblage was recognised as Cape Verde's first Unesco World Heritage Site.

Cidade Velha receives lots of tourists and has a couple of cafés and souvenir sellers specifically aimed at them, but it has so far, thankfully, escaped Disneyfication. It may be rich in historic sites, but it still functions as an ordinary village, where kids play football, women chat in doorways and fishermen pull their boats up onto the beach of black sand to divide out the catch.

The main square, which lies between the main road and the beach, is the site of one of Santiago's emblematic landmarks, the **Pelourinho** (pillory), a marble column variously described as a trading, torture or execution post for slaves. For such a grim monument, it's surprisingly decorative. Nearby is the village information centre which issues very basic local maps and tickets for entry to the fort and convent. Starting from here, it's possible to pick one's way around the Old Town, discovering ruins among the palm trees and banana plants.

The Glory Days of Ribeira Grande

Ribeira Grande was the Portuguese imperialists' first foothold in Africa, a welcome source of fresh water and food for Atlantic adventurers, and a notorious slave trading post. It fared extremely well in its early years, growing wealthy and being granted city status by the Pope. As Spanish-Portuguese territory, it was considered fair game by English seafarer Sir Francis Drake, who attacked with a thousand-strong force in 1585, plundering it with abandon and burning it to the ground. A devastating raid led by notorious French pirate Jacques Cassard in 1712 was the last straw, and the Portuguese set about moving their capital to Praia, risking malaria and other fatal ailments in the process.

The oldest structure is the **Igreja de Nossa Senhora do Rosário** (Church of Our Lady of the Rosary), built as a chapel in 1495 and sacked by Francis Drake, who stole its bell, in 1585. It was later rebuilt on a larger scale. Some of its tombs date back to the 16th and 17th centuries.

Almost as ancient is **Rua Banana**, the picturesque row of single-storey thatched cottages just below the church on the bank of the *ribeira*. Considered the oldest street in colonial Africa, these early

Rua Banana, one of the oldest streets in Cidade Velha

16th-century dwellings originally housed well-off Spanish and Portuguese traders; they are still in use as homes.

Further up the *ribeira* is the **Igreja-Convento de São Francisco** (Abbey of St Francis), founded in 1640 and wrecked by French pirates in 1712; it's in good enough shape, however, to be used as an exhibition space.

The **Cathedral**, constructed between 1556 and 1700, is in tatters; you can admire the remains of its bulk at the east end of the village. Presiding over the whole scene is the **Fortaleza Real de São Filipe**, built in 1587 after Drake and his men had done their worst, to prevent the wave of destruction being repeated. There are excellent views from its battlements, which still bristle with cannons.

Exploring Santiago

A main road runs north from Praia to São Domingos, through the island's lush, jaggedly mountainous interior to Assomada in the centre and Tarrafal in the north, then follows the north-east coast before turning south once again. Cobbled side roads wind their way up to hidden villages, and mountain tracks plunge down *ribeiras* to the coast, affording good opportunities for hikes and mountain bike treks.

At the small town of **São Domingos**, around 20 minutes north of Praia, is a craft centre (daily 9am–5pm) where you can usually see artisans including potters and weavers at work; its shop sells *pano* cloth, handmade hats and bags, and ceramic pots and vases in natural or glazed terracotta. Near here, in a vibrantly green valley, is the **Jardim Botânico Nacional** (National Botanic Garden), where native flora are studied and propagated.

Igreja de Nossa Senhora do Rosário

Overlooking this area are the stunning pinnacles, ridges and valleys of Santiago's **Serra de Pico de Antónia**.

Further north, around 37km (23 miles) from Praia, is the sizeable town of **Assomada**, famous for its large market, its *tabanca* tradition, and for being the former home of political activist Amílcar Cabral. The annual Tabanca Festival on the first Sunday in June involves dressing up as satirical characters (including royal personages, nurses and officials) and parading through the streets to the hooting of conch

Jardim Botânico Nacional

shells and the thumping of *surdo* drums. The history of *tabanca* is detailed at the **Museu da Tabanca** (Mon–Fri 9am–noon, 2–6pm; labels mostly in Portuguese) in nearby Chã de Tanque. On Assomada's main square, Praça de Gustavo Monteiro, the **Museu de Santa Catarina e de Norberto Tavares** is devoted to the history and people of Assomada and the Santa Catarina area, including the great singer-songwriter Norberto Tavares (1956–2010).

In the north of the island is the **Serra Malagueta**, a 2,600-hectare (6,400 acre) protected region of forested mountains harbouring endemic plants and birds. Its Casa do Ambiente (tourist centre; tel: 265 1211; Mon–Sat 8am–3.30pm, Sun 8.30am–2.30pm) can provide information for birdwatchers and hikers.

Beyond here, on the northwest coast, is **Tarrafal**, a laid-back seaside village with a sandy beach that's always busy at weekends. Tarrafal has a sinister history, as on its outskirts is a former concentration camp which was used between 1936 and 1974 by the PIDE (the dictator Salazar's notorious secret police) and their successors to incarcerate individuals who were considered enemies of the state of Portugal. Part of the camp now houses a museum, the **Museu da Resistência** (daily 8am–6pm).

FOGO

Fogo's unmistakable topography leaves you in no doubt that it is a young volcano. As you approach by plane, you're afforded astonishing views of its steep, conical shape. Unlike the other islands, whose eruptions petered out millennia ago, Fogo is alive and kicking – it has exploded five times in the last 200 years, most recently in 2014 – and it's topped by a giant caldera, 9km (5.5 miles) across. Contained within the crater is Cape Verde's loftiest peak, the 2,829-metre (9,279ft) Pico do Fogo, and surreal frozen seas of lava and ash.

São Filipe

Arranged over a steep slope on the west coast of the island, Fogo's compact capital, **São Filipe**, is one of Cape Verde's most pleasant towns. As you explore its cobbled streets, every corner offers a new view of terracotta-tiled rooftops, pastel-coloured façades and leafy squares, with a backdrop of sparkling sea. The Bandeira de São Filipe, one of Cape Verde's liveliest festivals, takes place here every 1 May when the cobbles in the city centre are sprinkled with sand in preparation for the traditional *cavalhadas* – thrilling horse races, contested at breakneck speed.

The town has a great many fine *sobrados* – colonial houses, usually two storeys high with a first-floor balcony of decorative timber and a pretty internal courtyard. Many of these have

Igreja Matriz de Nossa Senhora da Conceição

been restored in recent years, while others languish in elegant decay, awaiting their turn.

The attractive **Igreja Matriz de Nossa Senhora da Conceição** (parish church of the Immaculate Conception) was built towards the end of the 19th century. A *sobrado* near the church houses the **Museu Municipal de São Filipe** (District Museum; Mon–Fri 10am–3pm, Sat 10am–noon; labels mostly in Portuguese). Beautifully curated, this local history museum shows some fascinating documentary footage relating to the 1995 eruptions, and displays artefacts relating to Fogo's cultural heritage, such as a household shrine, an emigrant's trunk and an example of *pano* weaving. There's also a recreation of a *funco* – a hut built of lava blocks – and information on native flora and fauna.

Complementing the museum perfectly is the next-door **Casa de Memória** (Wed–Fri 10am–noon, or by appointment), a private collection of objects depicting the island's social history. Among the simple tools such as wooden bowls and granite mortars are imported items, including china plates from the Far East and a clock from the US, illustrating a fascination with the outside world. The centre also has a small library of books about Cape Verde, mostly in Portuguese or German.

Pieces of the past at the Casa de Memória

Parque Natural do Fogo

The crater at the centre of the island is a protected area, the **Parque Natural do Fogo**. A road leads into its heart, known as the **Chã das Caldeiras**, allowing you to

Volcanic desolation in the Parque Natural do Fogo

observe its eerie fields of dark, twisted, molten rock at close quarters. Some of Fogo's eruptions have caused lava to spill right down to the sea – 1680 and 1785 were particularly savage years – and in 2014 a kilometre-wide lava flow practically swallowed the headquarters of the park.

The lava is certainly impressive, but each eruption has brought new hardship to the islanders, devastating farmland and destroying buildings. A community of villagers live on the crater floor, where the soil is fertile and the water-retaining properties of the volcanic gravel allow a surprising variety of crops to be cultivated, including guava, apple, peach, pomegranate, fig and quince trees and, famously, grapevines and coffee bushes. The crater-dwellers were last forced to evacuate when the 2014 eruptions engulfed the entire crater with lava, ash and gravel, decimating the localities of Portela and Bangeira. The government has vowed to rebuild the settlements.

Hand-crafted souvenirs

In this region you may see brown-skinned, blond-haired children, a rarity in Cape Verde, offering tiny lava-stone *funcos* as souvenirs; these kids are the descendants of Fogo's pioneering wine-maker, François Montrond, a French duke who lived on the island in the 1870s.

The caldera has long attracted hikers who come to explore the crater floor and climb both **Pico Pequeno** (a small cone to the side of the main one), and **Pico do Fogo** (the main cone). However, the 2014 eruption has rendered caldera hikes a risky proposition for now.

Around Fogo

The remainder of Fogo is full of scenic drama, with the east coast a highlight for its spacious vistas, with lava streaking down from the cone and the dark sea foaming against jagged black rocks below. A ring road allows you to circumnavigate the island and admire its rustic heartlands. Some villages are perched right on the edge of lava fields. The steepness of the terrain has caused deep ravines to be carved out, producing dramatic waterfalls during the brief rainy season. Elsewhere, there are surprisingly lush plantations of bananas, papayas and vegetables, sustained by irrigation.

Near the town of **Mosteiros**, in the north of the island, are some intriguing rock formations, where layers of sedimentation appear to have collapsed into molten-looking shapes, while at **Ponta das Salinas** in the northwest there are some turbulent natural pools in the coastal lava.

BRAVA

Cape Verde's smallest inhabited island is an enchanting place which is rarely visited by tourists. The lack of an aerodrome presents something of an obstacle but a regular Fast Ferry catamaran service covers the 17km (10-mile) channel between Fogo and Brava five times a week. The journey time is around 40 minutes. When you reach Brava you'll be rewarded by stunning mountain scenery that's excellent for hiking, and encounters with supremely welcoming people.

There's a special relationship between Brava and Fogo, and legend has it that a volcanic tube connects the two islands beneath the ocean. Although that seems unlikely, over the centuries many people from Fogo have fled to Brava to escape eruptions and drought: Brava receives

An old lava flow meets the sea on the east coast of Fogo

more rain than any other Cape Verdean island, and is often cloaked in cloud.

There's also a special connection between Brava and the United States: practically every islander seems to have several American relatives. In the 19th century, American whaling boats used to stop here for provisions, and would make a point of recruiting Brava natives to their crews as they were known to be fearless seamen who would work hard for little pay. By the 1840s, nearly half of the New England whaling workers were from Brava, and many chose to settle permanently; there are particularly strong communities of Cape Verdeans from Brava in Boston. As a result, American accents can often be heard on Brava, photos of President Barack Obama are taped up in its bars, and American products regularly appear in its *mercearias* (village stores).

Storm clouds gather over the village of Furna

Vila Nova Sintra

From the port village of **Furna** where the boat docks, a steep, winding road rapidly climbs the 500 metres (1,600ft) or so up towards Brava's capital, **Vila Nova Sintra**. Hidden within a volcanic crater in order to escape the attentions of pirates, the small, quiet town of wide streets softened by flame trees, lobelia, hibiscus, bougainvillea and jasmine comes as a very pleasant surprise. Near the main square are a couple of *dragoeiras* (dragon trees), the strangely bewitched-looking species which also thrives on São Nicolau.

The square itself has a bandstand and a bust of Eugénio Tavares, one of Cape Verde's best-loved and most respected writers, who was born and lived on Brava. A highly romantic poet, journalist and composer of *mornas* in Creole, Tavares is

The only way to get to the tiny island of Brava is by ferry

considered one of the greatest modern interpreters of Cape Verdean culture. His house, on the southwest edge of town, is a museum, **Casa Museu Eugénio Tavares**. Furnished in period style are a living room, dining room, kitchen and bedrooms; several items, including trunks of books and papers, belonged to Tavares himself.

Exploring Brava

Brava's single main road continues uphill from Vila Nova Sintra into a rural hinterland where spiky agave plants stick out from cliffsides at jaunty angles, corn cobs are left to dry on cottage rooftops and villagers can be seen nudging cattle along cobbled tracks. Off the road are beautiful folded *ribeiras* and hidden farms. This is good birdwatching country, particularly for raptors, and the best way to appreciate the wildlife, and the glorious scenery, is on foot. Since the terrain is dauntingly steep, it's a good idea to take an *aluguer* up to a high starting point, and then make your way down with the help of a guide or a good map.

At a fork in the road, the main drag swings round the island's lofty central peak, **Monte Fontainhas** (976 metres/ 3,202ft), to the hamlet of **Cachaço**. The other road leads off down to **Fajã d'Água** on the northwest coast. The steep downhill approach to the village is breathtaking: this is perhaps the most beautifully located settlement in the country, nestled on a perfect bay fringed with dark stones, its row of palm-shaded fishermen's houses dwarfed by a towering mountain backdrop.

SÃO VICENTE

The jewel of São Vicente is Mindelo, Cape Verde's second city. Elegantly laid out on a beautiful bay ringed with mountains, it has a cosmopolitan atmosphere and a hectic cultural scene – many musicians, writers, artists and thinkers hail from here, ocean-going yachts call in on their way to the Caribbean, and Cape Verde's biggest and glitziest carnival is held here every February.

A healthy island

'The salubrity of St Vincent is very superior to any of the other islands,' wrote John Rendall, Her Majesty Queen Victoria's British Consul in Cape Verde, in 1851. At the time, the health risks in the tropics were considerable, and Rendall considered fever-riddled Praia 'more fatal than the coast of Africa'.

The rest of São Vicente doesn't really live up to Mindelo's promise – it's relentlessly arid, with denuded mountains and just a few ragged villages – but off-road explorations reveal some interesting subtleties, from desert-adapted plants to seldom-visited beaches. Sadly, perhaps, parts of this little-known hinterland are soon to be engulfed by development,

Mindelo's colourful waterfront

when the island's gleaming new airport begins to receive international flights.

Mindelo

First discovered by Portuguese explorer Diogo Afonso in 1462, São Vicente remained largely uninhabited for the next 300 years or so. During this time it was the occasional hangout of corsairs, pirates and foreign squadrons, who came here to hunt goats and donkeys, roasting or smoking the meat and using the skins to make bottles.

It was only in the early 19th century that the British spotted the potential of the spectacular harbour at **Mindelo**. This was the time when coal-fired steamships were taking over from sail, and Britain's mail-carrying ocean liners were leading the way, slashing travel times from Europe to the Americas and Asia in half. In 1838, the British gained permission from the Portuguese governors to bring shipments of Welsh coal to São Vicente to sell to passing ships. This was the start of a highly lucrative refuelling business. Initially, the coal was stored on floating barges. Later it was brought onto land and wheeled to the seafront by railroad; a section of the track has been preserved as a monument near the ferry terminal.

By the 1850s, several British coaling companies were operating in Mindelo; some of their quayside offices are still standing. The boom years lasted until the turn of the century, when the Portuguese made the mistake of raising duties to such an extent that traders and factories upped and left. When oil took over from coal, the Canaries and Dakar were better placed to refuel the transatlantic vessels.

Today, Mindelo is confidently prosperous once again, as its quality of life attracts a wide variety of businesses. Recent urban regeneration has restored some of its squares with new

Carnival

Mindelo's pre-Lenten carnival is inspired by Brazil's Mardi Gras. For four days, the town is engulfed by parades and concerts which, though modest in scale compared to, say, Rio or São Paulo, lack nothing in cheerful exuberance. Dressing up is an essential part of proceedings, and many spectators join in by wearing horror masks, silly wigs or full-blown fancy dress. Each neighbourhood has its own carnival troupe which compete for accolades including best float and best music. The troupes always include scores of *mandingas* – young men kitted out as African tribal warriors in shiny black body paint and grass skirts, brandishing spears – and samba girls in colourful satin outfits with feathered headdresses and glittery make-up. People of all ages, from toddlers to grandmothers, take part. *Batucadas* (drum bands) clatter through the streets and the costumed paraders dance like there's no tomorrow.

cobbles and revitalised the façades of its historic buildings with vibrant colours.

Mindelo is very easy to explore on foot. **Rua de Lisboa**, at its heart, leads down from the late 19th-century **Palâcio do Povo** (Palace of the People), an imposing local government building which sometimes hosts exhibitions. Initially a single-storey building, and dismissed by one colonial governor for being

Mindelo's carnival is a riot of colour and music

unacceptably commonplace, it acquired the added grandeur of a first floor in the 1930s. The newly independent republic's first prime minister, Pedro Pires, gave an address from here in July 1975.

Halfway down Rua de Lisboa is the **Mercado Municipal**, a spotless market hall piled high with luscious fruit and vegetables, including huge marrows, melons and bananas from Santo Antão. Nearby is the tiny **Café Lisboa**, a quirky, open-all-hours meeting place where locals engage in animated discussion over stiff little cups of coffee, flaky *pasteis de nata* and glasses of *aguardente*.

At the seafront end of the street, in a former post office building, is the **Alliance Française**, the Mindelo branch of France's extensive West African network of cultural centres. Opposite this is one of Mindelo's older buildings, the very solid Alfândega Velha (Old Customs House), completed in 1860 and now home to the **Centro Cultural do Mindelo** (CCM; Mon–Thu 9am–noon and 3–9pm, Fri 9am–12.30pm, Sat 10am–noon and 5–9pm, Sun 5–9pm; free), with an exhibition space, bookshop, gift shop and a programme of talks and films, most in Portuguese or Creole.

Overlooking the new **marina** nearby is a large sculpture of an eagle on a heap of rocks, which is a monument to Sacadura Cabral and Gago Coutinho, who in 1922 became the first aviators to cross the South Atlantic. Mindelo was one of the stops on their voyage, which started in Lisbon in March and ended in Rio de Janeiro in June.

The seafront **Avenida da República** has the look of a Mediterranean corniche, with shady palm trees and old merchants' houses painted in glorious shades of yellow, blue, turquoise and ochre. A large statue of Diogo Afonso stands among the fishing boats parked on the working beach, **Praia dos Botes**, while nearby is the **Capitania dos Portos**, a scaled-down replica of Portugal's Torre de Belém, with a small maritime museum inside and pleasant views from the roof. Next door is the lively **Mercado de Peixe** (fish market), with heaps of shining mackerel, octopus and tuna on offer and a flurry of fish-cleaning going on. Inland from here is the **Praça da Estrela**, an open square with a souvenir market decorated with tile murals depicting scenes from the island's history.

Intricately woven pano cloth in the Casa de Senador Augusto Vera-Cruz

Heading back towards Rua Lisboa, you pass through Mindelo's oldest quarter, a tight grid of cobbled streets leading to the **Câmara Municipal** (town hall). The 19th-century parish church, **Igreja de Nossa Senhora da Luz** (Our Lady of Light) has no fewer than three altars to the Virgin, and a ceiling painting of her ascending into heaven, buoyed up by puffy clouds.

The view from Praia de Laginha towards Santo Antão

Heading north through Mindelo's main shopping district, you come to Praça de Amílcar Cabral, more commonly known as **Praça Nova**, a leafy square where locals come to stroll and socialise. At one end is the faintly Art Nouveau Quiosque Praça Nova, an essential drinks stop, and at the other is the **Casa do Senador Augusto Vera-Cruz** (House of Senator Augusto Vera-Cruz; Mon–Fri 9am–noon, and 3–6pm, Sat 9am–1pm). This elegant, Regency-style building was a society club in the 1930s and a radio station from the 1950s to the 1980s; it now houses a small but interesting exhibition of rustic ceramics, *pano* weaving, tapestries, musical instruments, and artefacts connected with the building's history.

Along **Avenida Marginal** on the north side of town is the smart, liner-shaped ferry terminal; Porto Grande, the container port, its walls decorated with striking environmental awareness murals; and **Fortim d'El Rei**, a ruined citadel with fine views over the city. Reached via Rua Alto Fortim, northwest of

Terracotta modeller at work

Praça Nova, this site has been earmarked for conversion into a resort complex including a boutique hotel, casino and upmarket restaurants.

Beyond the port is **Praia de Laginha**, the best beach close to the city centre, with pleasant sand, safe swimming and views of the docks, Santo Antão and the shell-shaped islet of Ilhéu dos Passaros.

In addition to the Centro Cultural and the Casa do Senador Augusto Vera-Cruz, Mindelo has several other art and craft exhibitions and workshops, including the **Associação Escola Terracota**, a workshop in a dilapidated building on the hill close to the ferry terminal, where artisans make beautiful figurines and pots from recycled terracotta tiles. Tapestry artist Joana Pinto and celebrated painter Kiki Lima both have studios near Praça Nova.

Good shops for distinctive souvenirs include the **Akuaba** gallery shop on Rua de Lisboa, which sells cloth and antiquities from the African mainland; **Arte Criola** on Rua 5 de Julho for a jumble of ceramics, tin-can cars and bottles of *grogue*, and **Atelier de Violão Aniceto Gomes** in Monte Sossego district for handmade guitars and *cavaquinhos*. Live music is also a Mindelo speciality – try Chez Loutcha on Rua de Côco or Café Algarve on Rua de Lisboa.

Exploring São Vicente
Inland São Vicente has an austere appeal which is best appreciated by getting off-road. Palm trees and vegetable plots battle

against the drought-stricken *ribeiras* which lie in the shadow of the Madeiral mountains, and groves of acacia trees bring much-needed colour to the scene.

São Pedro, at the west end of the island, has little to offer beyond its sandy beach, right under the approach to the Cesária Évora airport with a large bronze statue of the São Vicente-born "Barefoot Diva", but the region southeast of here has a wild drama, with beautiful, empty beaches of finely crushed white coral, set in an amphitheatre of ancient, russet-coloured volcanoes. Here and there you may see desert melons, which look much like fishing floats tangled up in an old net, or heather-coloured succulents, which used to be used to make natural dyes. Ospreys hover over the water, and on a clear day you can see across to the uninhabited islands of Branco and Santa Luzia, with the peaks of São Nicolau in the far distance.

Mindelo harbour, as seen from Monte Verde

Calhau, a fishing village on the east coast, looks very jaunty as you approach it from the south, its splash of bright orange and yellow houses contrasting sharply with the bright blue bay. Just north of here is a volcanic cone and a long, dark beach, **Praia Grande**, which leads to **Baía das Gatas**, home to a large new resort development and an annual music festival. Inland from here is **Monte Verde**, São Vicente's highest point, which is a national park.

SANTO ANTÃO

Santo Antão is an enigmatic gem of an island, its south and west sides forbiddingly barren and brown, its spine frequently blanketed in cloud, and its northwest side a vertiginous riot of lush green ridges and valleys. Remote and little affected by modern life, there's an appealing innocence to the place; it's also incredibly scenic, making it Cape Verde's most attractive destination for hardy hikers.

Porto Novo to Ribeira Grande

The 30–60-minute ferry crossing to Santo Antão from São Vicente is a much cheaper journey than any of Cape Verde's internal flights, and faster overall, taking airport waiting time into account, but the channel can be choppy. There's always a crowd of vehicles awaiting the ferries at **Porto Novo** on Santo Antão's southern coast; this purposeful little port town also has a few bars and vendors selling drinks and snacks.

Fortune-telling

On 12 June, the eve of the Feast of Santo António, the single girls of the Paúl Valley break an egg into a glass of water and leave it in the moonlight. Next day, the shape of the white tells their fortune – a boat shape spells emigration, and a bridal veil means a wedding is on the cards.

The mountain road from Porto Novo to Ribeira Grande is one of Cape Verde's most unforgettable scenic routes. It hairpins up the mountain and into the clouds at a dizzying rate, carving through brown *ribeiras* where little grows apart from wild aloe vera and small acacias. A new coastal road connecting Porto Novo to Paúl was built in 2009 but the views are less impressive.

At the top, the atmosphere suddenly cools and becomes calm, grey and alpine. Warmly wrapped villagers appear clutching wheels of wet, creamy goat's cheese, which they sell to passers-by. If the cloud lifts, you can look down through lichen-clad

Porto Novo is on the arid side of the island

pine trees to the floor of the **Cova de Paúl**, a crater patch-worked with fields. North of here the road begins a gasp-inducing series of twists and turns as it tumbles along ridges and down mountainsides in the direction of Ribeira Grande. Crofts surrounded by banana trees, cassava and sugar-cane plants cling to steep spots which appear impossible to reach, and villagers lead donkeys along narrow paths.

At the other end of the road, the old town of **Ribeira Grande**, locally referred to as the *povoação* (village), consists of a row of houses on a seafront cliff, with a tight jumble of old buildings, including a large parish church, **Igreja de Nossa Senhora do Rosário** (Our Lady of the Rosary) sheltering behind them. Ribeira Grande was the capital of Cape Verde's Barlovento islands in the late 19th and early 20th centuries, but is now decidedly faded.

Exploring Santo Antão

Ponta do Sol on the north coast, a scenically impressive drive west along the cliff road from Ribeira Grande, is a popular base for visitors. This quiet fishing town has wide streets with some fine old buildings, several laidback *pensões* and restaurants, and one of the most pleasant craft galleries on the islands, **Artesanato Eki Eko**, selling Santo Antão's distinctive pictures made from collages of sand, dried leaves and bark, along with ceramics from São Vicente and Sal, pretty necklaces, mobiles and baskets, and local produce including *grogue*, *pontche*, coffee and jam. Hikers using Ponta do Sol as a starting point are spoilt for choice, but one great option is to head west to the stunningly picturesque cliff-hugging village of **Fontainhas**.

The area east of Ribeira Grande also has some superb spots for hikers and mountain bikers. One easy and highly rewarding location to try is the **Vale do Paúl**, a dazzlingly lush valley which opens onto the sea at the village of **Vila das Pombas**. Stuffed with banana, mango and papaya trees, flame trees, poinsettias and vegetable plots, it offers easy, pleasant walking. You can also visit a traditional *trapiche* (sugarmill) to watch grogue being distilled, and maybe try a shot. It's possible to walk all the way to Vila das

Lush vegetation in the Vale do Paúl

Isolated crofts on São Nicolau

Pombas from Cova de Paúl, a thrilling but testing all-day hike with extremely steep sections.

The west side of Santo Antão is so mountainous and arid that it's surprising that anybody lives there. With a 4x4 – and plenty of time – you can explore its rocky tracks, perhaps heading for the delightfully peaceful coastal hamlet of **Tarrafal de Monte Trigo**. Here, it's possible to go out fishing by night, hauling in the catch by hand.

SÃO NICOLAU

Although sometimes overlooked by visitors who don't have time to see more than one or two islands, São Nicolau is immensely rewarding to explore. A great part of its attraction lies in the fact that so few foreigners make it here, so it remains thoroughly unspoilt: self-sufficient hikers and mountain bikers could easily spend several enjoyable days trekking through its mountainous terrain. But what makes São Nicolau unique is its cultural heritage: it is the former home of a leading academic institution, the Seminário da Ribeira Brava, which trained some of the island's finest minds in the late 19th and early 20th centuries. The legacy of this time continues to colour the atmosphere of the island community, and the capital, Vila da Ribeira Brava, is vaguely reminiscent of an old university town.

Though one of the islands which makes the fewest concessions to tourists, São Nicolau nonetheless is set up with neatly kept *pensões* and friendly restaurants where you can tuck into deliciously fresh fish or *môdje*, a favourite stew, generally made with vegetables and goat meat.

Vila da Ribeira Brava

Like Vila Nova Sintra on Brava, São Nicolau's capital was founded in a peaceful location out of sight of the coast, as a ruse to foil pirates. As such, it has the atmosphere of a secret

Es Caminho Longe: the Long Road to São Tomé

São Nicolau receives more rainfall than many of the islands, but it is very isolated, and many of the islanders are poor. During the devastating droughts of the 19th and 20th centuries, a large number of them left their homes and families to emigrate to the *roças* (cocoa plantations) of São Tomé and Príncipe in the Gulf of Guinea on the promise of a good life and a generous salary. Neither of these materialised, however, thanks to the machinations of the greedy and ruthless Portuguese colonial elite.

Too poor to afford the voyage home, many São Nicolauans ended up life-long exiles, and they and their descendants remain on the islands of São Tomé and Príncipe to this day. It was these tragic circumstances which inspired the sorrowful *morna* entitled Sodade, written by São Nicolau-born composer Armando Zeferino Soares, and made famous by Césaria Évora.

oasis. The Ribeira Brava Valley is particularly attractive – a deep ravine overlooked by towering volcanic slopes, dotted with crosses, a legacy of the community's staunch Catholic heritage. Pleasant colonial buildings are crammed along the valley, with lovely views from the higher streets.

The town's main focus is the **Terreiro**, or main square, which has a charming period feel, with lantern street lights and a formal garden in which stand a fountain and a bust of Dr Júlio José Dias, the benefactor who donated his home to be the Seminário. Dominating the square is the 17th-century church, **Igreja**

Inside the 17th-century Igreja de Nossa Senhora do Rosário

de Nossa Senhora do Rosário (Our Lady of the Rosary), whose bells are banged by hand on Sundays to call well-groomed locals to mass. The interior is a grand, baroque confection with a rather mawkish modern painting of the Virgin and Child on the ceiling. The church escaped pirate raids so effectively that it retains several treasures, including a magnificent gold chalice; this is usually locked away, but it may soon be displayed in a new museum of heritage and sacred art at Calajão, south of town.

The elegant *sobrados* surrounding the Terreiro include an old guildhall and former slaughterhouse. The whole area becomes a scene of joyful colour and noise every February for the pre-Lenten carnival, or Festas do Rei Momo, which is smaller than Mindelo's carnival, but every bit as fun.

Near the Terreiro is the spotless **Mercado Municipal** (town market), where women sell tidy piles of carrots, potatoes and squashes. There are two smaller squares near the riverbed, one containing the **Câmara Municipal** (town hall), the post office and a 1950s public water point. It's close to the birthplace of Baltasar Lopes da Silva (1907–89), a famous Cape Verdean novelist and linguist, who is honoured with a statue depicting him as a rather avuncular figure, standing with his hands in his pockets and a book under one arm. The other square, right beside the river-bed, has a café and a bandstand, and is named after Monsenhor António Bouças, founder of the Seminário.

The **Seminário**, a simple, rectangular building with tall windows, is on the other side of the *ribeira*, towards the edge of town; these days it's used for catechism classes and is not open to the public, although it's possible to admire it from the outside. In its heyday it served not only as a Catholic seminary but also provided the likes of Lopes da Silva with a general classical education.

Trapiches

São Nicolao's sugar cane is cut in February, ready to be crushed by the traditional *trapiches* (sugarmills), which are either animal-driven or engine-powered. The juice is then left to ferment before being distilled into *grogue* using a furnace fuelled by sugar-cane leaves. Nothing is wasted: animals chew on the chaff, and the ash is used as fertiliser.

One of São Nicolau's most pleasant walks is the 4km (2.5-mile) uphill trek out of town, following a cobbled track along the Ribeira Grande to Cachaço, the gateway to the Parque Natural de Monte Gordo. This route takes you past terraced farmland, swathes of wild aloe vera, characterful villages and a *grogue* distillery. Fruit trees fill the dips and the

Using a trapiche to crush sugar cane for grogue, Queimadas

whole valley echoes with the calls of birds, donkeys, dogs and cockerels, amplified by the steep sides. Towards the top, the track is dizzyingly steep, with fabulous views. Finally you reach the **Capela de Nossa Senhora de Monte Cintinha**, a mountain chapel commissioned by Canon Bouças in 1919, with a simple but charming interior and a garden planted with hibiscus bushes.

Exploring São Nicolau

Second only to Santo Antão's mountain road for scenic drama is the road from Vila da Ribeira Brava to Tarrafal on the west coast. This starts by following the coast along a cliff road, with treacherous white surf pounding the rocks below, and then turns inland.

A detour leads to **Queimadas**, a pretty clutch of cottages on a steep hillside dotted with wild aloe vera, with a *grogue* distillery at the bottom. Uphill from here are the twin villages

Dragon trees

The sap of the *dragoeira*, a symbol of São Nicolau, is considered a powerful cure-all, especially when mixed with *grogue*. This custom has caused the depletion of these trees in the past, but they're now protected. An illustration of a *dragoeira* appears on the 1,000 escudo note.

of **Fajã de Baixo** and **Fajã de Cima**, perched in a farming region where the well-irrigated fields burst with healthy crops including maize, passion fruit, guavas, avocados, coffee, tomatoes and onions.

The higher you climb, the cooler the air becomes, and the roadside village of **Cachaço**, in the shadow of São Nicolau's volcanic peak, Monte Gordo, is surrounded by bean fields, some of them with strange, spiky-looking *dragoeiras* (dragon trees) guarding them like scarecrows.

A walking track leads from Cachaço into the **Parque Natural de Monte Gordo**; on the way you pass its visitor centre, the Casa do Ambiente (Mon–Fri 8.30am–3.30pm), where you can request a free guide to show you the various trails and point out plant and wildlife species of interest. All the trails have a good variety of flora and fauna to admire; some are steep. The park is a mixed-use region in which farmers still cultivate fruit and vegetables, but conservationists have been working with them to help safeguard native endemic plants against soil erosion and the threat presented by invasive non-native species.

Beyond Cachaço, the road rounds the peak of Monte Gordo to course through an area which is considerably drier. There are panoramic views from here right down the valley to Vila da Ribeira Brava. The road continues steeply downward through a parched, russet and ginger landscape of ancient lava fields to **Tarrafal**, São Nicolau's main port. Larger and more animated than the capital, especially whenever a ferry or fishing boat rolls into the dock, Tarrafal is nonetheless a thoroughly easy-going little town with a permanent but surprisingly acceptable whiff of tuna hanging in the air. It has two beaches, both with dark sand and clear water – one is used by the fishermen, and the other is good for swimming or playing football. Another beach, **Baía de Baixo da Rocha**, with a remote, castaway feel and pale sand, is a rather arduous two-hour walk away along the rocky coast to the south.

North of Tarrafal there's more lonely coastal scenery to explore, including the black sands of **Barril**, which are said to cure rheumatism, and the intriguing **Rotxa Skribis**, rocks which look as they have been inscribed with writing.

In the remote arm of the island east of Vila da Ribeira Brava, the road ends at **Juncalinho**, where there's a natural rock swimming pool with lovely clear water.

Local teenagers by the fishing beach in Tarrafal

WHAT TO DO

Cape Verde offers plenty of options to those who would like to do more than just relax on a lovely beach. Sal and Boa Vista both have world-class conditions for watersports, and the mountainous islands of Santiago, Fogo, Brava, Santo Antão and São Nicolau are laced with inspiring hiking trails. Other highlights for the active traveller include the opportunity to observe native birds, turtles, whales and tropical fish in the wild, and to soak up the islands' unmistakable music in local clubs and bars.

SPORTS AND OUTDOOR ACTIVITIES

Watersports

Thanks to its ferocious northeasterly winds and dazzling waves, Sal became a **windsurfing** hangout long before it was discovered by more sedentary sunseekers. In recent years, many professional windsurfers and kitesurfers have given Sal the thumbs up; some have even settled here. One of the best known is American-born Josh Ângulo, a former world champion who is married to a Cape Verdean and runs a successful local windsurfing operation, Angulo Cabo Verde Surf Center (www.angulocaboverde.com).

Sal's weather conditions are reliably exciting – force five winds and a 4-metre (13ft) swell are commonplace at Ponta Preta, northwest of Santa Maria, in the winter months. However, even on calmer days, skilled windsurfers will normally find a gust to power them along.

For beginners, Santa Maria Bay on Sal is usually perfectly manageable – it's protected, with a steady offshore

Skimboarders on Praia de Santa Maria, Sal

Sal has excellent conditions for windsurfing

wind. Estoril Bay near Sal Rei on Boa Vista is also recommended for its shallow water and offshore wind. For **kitesurfing**, the best spot is Serra Negra (sometimes called Kite Beach or Shark Bay), northwest of Santa Maria.

Santa Maria and Sal Rei have a number of training bases with good gear to hire, including Angulo on Praia António Sousa (www.angulocaboverde.com), Surf Zone at the Morabeza Beach Club (www.surfcaboverde.com) and Boa Vista Wind Club on Tortuga Beach (www.boavista windclub.com). If you are highly experienced and intend to explore some out-of-the-way spots, it's advisable to bring your own kit.

For **surfing**, conditions on the islands aren't quite as good as elsewhere in the Atlantic, but the Tarrafal area of northern Santiago sees enough decent waves to attract a few boardriders. There's also some surf on the south and southwest coasts of Sal and the south coast of São Vicente. You can hire boards at windsurfing stations.

Scuba-diving and **snorkelling** are possible, in theory, in many parts of the country, as long as you're equipped to deal with challenging currents and are aware that there's no recompression chamber on the islands. Santa Maria has several scuba operations, such as Cabo Verde Diving (www.caboverdediving.net) and Orca Dive Club (www.orca-dive club-caboverde.com), which run PADI courses and visits to sites all around the coast, including coral gardens, lava caves and wrecks. Once underwater you can expect to see a wealth of tropical fish, plus crustaceans and moray eels. If you're lucky, you may meet a loggerhead turtle, or hear the song of a humpback whale. Dolphins also patrol these waters. Maio's treacherous reefs and sandbanks have caused the untimely end of many ships; divers can explore some of them with the Maio Pluf diving centre (tel: 971 0006, www.maiocv.com).

Hiking

A large number of people visit Cape Verde specifically to go **hiking**. Challenging trails through breathtaking mountain scenery can be found on Santo Antão, São Nicolau, Santiago, Fogo and Brava, and many of these can be explored independently with the help of a good map (see page 126).

A spectacular backdrop for a hike on Fogo

However, you are likely to have a more illuminating experience in the hands of a good guide, which can be arranged by Cape Verde Trekking (www.capeverde trekking.com) who offer a range of treks, including tailor-made tours on Santiago, Santo Antão, São Nicolau, Brava and Fogo islands. Be warned that some islands also have a few would-be freelance guides who lack adequate experience. Your guide should be able to advise on the best routes for the season and weather conditions, assess your pace, and arrange any extras you might need such as camping equipment, meals or a donkey to carry your gear. They will also act as an interpreter, both of the local culture and of the landscape.

Wildlife Watching

The waters around the islands are visited by five species of **turtle** – green, leatherback, olive ridley, hawksbill and loggerhead – all of which are endangered. Conservation officers have been making a concerted attempt to safeguard the loggerheads which lay their eggs on the beaches of Boa Vista, Maio and Sal between late May and early October. **Dolphins** are regularly seen in Cape Verdean waters, and humpback whales are seasonal visitors: they have been known to calve here in the spring. SOS Tartarugas (tel: 974 5020, www.turtlesos.org) on Sal organise wildlife tours for those interested in seeing native species, particularly turtles, in their natural habitat. You can also support their conservation program by adopting a hatchling turtle.

Grey-headed kingfisher

Island hotspots for **bird-watchers** include Santiago, Fogo and Brava, home to frigate birds, raptors and the grey-headed kingfisher (known locally as the *passarinha*), an emblematic bird which has adapted to its environment by eating insects and small reptiles rather than fish. São Vicente and São Nicolau are home to a rare endemic bird, the neglected kestrel, and Raso, an uninhabited islet between the two, has an extremely rare bird named after it: the Raso lark.

Off-Road Adventures

Since Cape Verde's road network is severely limited, you miss a great deal if travelling by car or minibus. **Off-roading** can be a real revelation, particularly on islands like São Vicente and Sal, whose landscapes seem depressingly barren from the road; explore in more detail and you will discover dramatic vistas, hidden beaches

Quad-biking on Sal

and interesting desert-adapted plants. Sabura Adventures (www.sabura-adventures.com) is highly recommended for its illuminating and surprisingly comfortable 4x4 tours of São Vicente and Santo Antão.

Several companies, including Barracuda Tours (www. barracudatours.com) on Sal and Boa Vista, run **quad bike** tours, an interesting way to see the desert, though dusty and potentially damaging to the environment. Cabo Verde No Limits on Santo Antão (www.caboverdenolimits.com) organises other adventure activities such as **climbing** and **canyoning**.

For the keen and fit, **mountain biking** is a superb option. Riding over rocky or cobbled tracks in hot, windy

Football on the beach

weather can be exhausting, but if you choose your routes carefully you're likely to find the stunning scenery ample compensation. With your own wheels, the main limit to your options is which islands you can get to – it's easier to carry a bike as baggage on ferries than on internal flights. Companies such as Cape Verde Trekking (www.cabo verde-trekking.com) organise interesting mountain bike tours. It's also possible to hire mountain bikes through hotels on Sal, Boa Vista, São Vicente or Santo Antão.

Local Pastimes

Football is a national obsession in Cape Verde. Followed and played by women and girls just as much as by males of all ages, the game holds so much fascination that everything stops when a key match is being shown on television. Any team featuring a Cape Verdean, West African, Portuguese or Brazilian player is considered worth following; Manchester United, for whom Praia-born Portuguese footballer Nani plays, is a favourite. The sports pitch – whether it's a rectangle of floodlit concrete or just part of the beach – takes pride of place in every town, and the spirit of the match spills over to bars decked out with team regalia, with table football games set up outside.

Wherever there's a shady square or doorstep, you're likely to see a knot of Cape Verdean men indulging in a card game or one of their other favourite pastimes, **oril**, the local version of Africa's ubiquitous game of holes and seeds. It's a fast-moving test of skill in which each of two opponents takes it in turn to move handfuls of pebbles around a wooden board, with a view to capturing all the pieces.

SHOPPING

As a rule, Cape Verdeans shop out of necessity rather than as a pastime. Markets and *mercearias* (grocery shops) are as much a place to pick up the latest gossip as to stock up on fresh produce and other essentials. A relatively recent, and conspicuous, addition to the shopping options in most towns and villages are the Chinese-run general stores which are often simply called *Loja*, the Portuguese name for a shop or store. Despite the fact that Chinese importers have jeopardised local manufacturers' livelihoods by flooding Africa with cheap merchandise, their shops are hugely popular with poorer families in Cape Verde, as they're an accessible source of affordable (though rather shoddy) shoes, clothes and household goods.

For visitors, the most varied shopping is to be found in **Santa Maria**

African souvenirs in Santa Maria

Terracotta pots at the Escola de Olaria on Boa Vista

on Sal. Many places stay open late, sometimes until midnight, and prices are generally rather high. The village has been overtaken with souvenir shops; some of these are disappointing, but the best sell attractive handmade jewellery, ceramics and trinkets. You'll also see appealingly presented bags of coffee, jars of jam, and bottles of *grogue* and *pontche*, and clothing such as swimwear and surf gear with local branding. Boa Vista caters for souvenir-hunters, too, with pricey bead jewellery, shell mobiles and other oddments, sold in and around the main square in Sal Rei.

Two of the best places to buy **crafts** direct from the makers are the artisans' centre in São Domingos, Santiago, which is good for traditional weaving and ceramics, and the Associação Escola Terracota in Mindelo, São Vicente (see page 70), where craftsmen create rustic terracotta figures and pots. Mindelo is also the place to buy a handmade guitar, a hand-woven wall-hanging, or some interesting African artefacts, from cheap beads to spectacular masks. Santo Antão and São Nicolau have one excellent craft shop each: Eki Eko in Ponta do Sol (see page 74) and Gaia in Vila da Ribeira Brava.

If, like many visitors, you find yourself falling in love with Cape Verde's evocative **music**, then CDs make an excellent souvenir. They cost more on the islands than you might expect (€15–20 for an album is typical), but you'll find a wider selection of material by local artists here than outside the country, even online. Harmonia music shops are excellent for CDs by artists from Cape Verde and elsewhere in Africa: you'll find branches in the public areas of the airports on Sal and Boa Vista, in Praia, and in Mindelo. Music shops, like gift shops, tend to stay open late in the evening.

The shops in the public areas of the **airports** on Sal and Boa Vista are also worth a browse for gifts such as clothing,

Ten Classic Albums

If you'd like to start your own Cape Verdean CD collection, you can't go wrong with these. All are on international release.

Mayra Andrade, *Lovely Difficult* (RCA Victor/Sony Music, 2013). Charming songs in four languages, with international influences.

Baú, *Ilha Azul* (Lusafrica, 2006). Baú is one of Mindelo's most celebrated guitarists.

Teofilo Chantre, *Viajá* (Lusafrica, 2007). Evocative and romantic singer from São Nicolau.

Cesária Évora, *Miss Perfumado* (Lusafrica, 1992). Includes her world-famous rendition of *Sodade*.

Ferro Gaita, *Rei de Funaná* (Lusafrica, 2003). Hugely popular as a live act, theses guys really are the kings of *funaná*.

Ildo Lobo, *Incondicional* (Lusafrica, 2005). A highly charismatic *morna* singer from Sal.

Suzanna Lubrano, *Saida* (Mass Appeal, 2008). Funky diva of *kizomba*, Cape Verdean zouk.

Gabriela Mendes, *Tradição* (Nocturne, 2007). Catchy *coladêra* numbers from a well-established singer.

Simentera, *Simentera* (Piranha, 2000). Highly respected band, founders of Praia's Quintal da Música.

Tcheka, *Dor de mar* (Lusafrica, 2011). A blend of various Cape Verdean genres and music forms.

The house band at a bistro in Mindelo

bottles of grogue, jewellery and gifts decorated with turtles. Sal's duty-free shopping area is rather overpriced.

ENTERTAINMENT

Cape Verdean entertainment and nightlife is focused around drinking, conversation and music – either listening to it, dancing or taking part. With its lilting melodies and hot-blooded guitar rhythms, traditional Cape Verdean music sounds more Latin than African – in fact, drums, the backbone of many styles of West African music, are little used except by carnival bands. Instead, the tempo is set by rolling chords on the *violão* (guitar), overlaid with rapid strumming on the *cavaquinho*, a small, high-pitched, four-string guitar which looks endearingly like a toy. Providing the melody, gypsy-style, are a solo singer or a virtuoso *rabeca* (violin). Some bands also include clarinet, saxophone, piano, and traditional percussion such as *racordai*, *güiro* and *reco-reco* (shakers and scrapers). Cape Verdean musicians tend to be extremely versatile, switching from one instrument to another and taking turns to pick up the lead.

Cape Verde has several distinctive musical styles of which the best known, and most romantic, is **morna** – the poignant, poetic ballads which express the essence of *sodade*, a nostalgic longing for home and for lost love. These evocative songs have many exponents, male and female, but were made world-famous by Mindelo-born diva Cesária Évora (1941–2011).

Other musical styles are more danceable. Crank up the beat of a *morna* and you end up with a **coladêra**, a funky, hip-wiggling dance that sometimes incorporates Latin and Caribbean rhythms such as samba, merengue and zouk. Couples dance together, ballroom-style.

Other strictly Creole dances include *batuko* and *funaná*, both originating from Santiago. **Batuko** is accompanied by the *cimbôa*, a local instrument consisting of a resonating gourd with a rod and a string, played with a bow. Similar to a West African dance, women in big skirts join together in a circle, clapping, stamping and beating out the rhythm on their thighs, and taking it in turns to leap into the centre for a frenetic solo. **Funaná** also has a fast, powerful pulse and is danced in couples, with plenty of sensual body contact. The melody is played on a *gaita* (accordion), while a *ferrinho* (metal scraper) provides percussion.

Master of morna

Eugénio Tavares (1867–1930) is such a highly revered figure in Cape Verdean culture that he is honoured with a portrait on the 2,000 escudo note, along with a quote from *Morna da Aguada*, a characteristically passionate song about '*martirio de amor*' – the martyrdom of love.

Young carnival-goer, Mindelo

Your best chance of seeing traditional dances is to be in Cape Verde for a saint's day festival (see page 96): every island has several of these. Some tourist hotels also lay on Creole nights with music and dancing. Traditional music is easier to find – bands regularly play in hotels, restaurants and bars (particularly in Santa Maria and Mindelo), in town-centre bandstands on Sundays, and at the music festivals which crop up each year. DJs at the clubs in Santa Maria, Mindelo and Praia play a mixture of local sounds and reggae, rap, hip-hop and house. Praia's legendary live music venue, **Quintal da Música** on Avenida Amílcar Cabral (tel: 261 1679), has sessions most nights of the week. The most enchanting way to enjoy music, however, is to happen across a *tocatina* – an informal jam session – which might take place in any bar, at any time. There are music schools in Mindelo and Espargos, so these are good places to keep your ears open.

CHILDREN'S CAPE VERDE

Portuguese and Italian families have been spending their holidays in Cape Verde for many years, but dedicated family facilities are still rather rare. Some beach hotels – particularly the large all-inclusive resorts – have carers for toddlers and activity organisers for older kids, but many speak little English. It's also worth bearing in mind that in winter, the sea is usually too rough for swimming, and pools are often chilly.

The islands are best suited to self-sufficient families who are keen on walking or watersports. Although some of Cape Verde's mountain hikes would be too tough for young legs, a competent guide should be able to help you plan a manageable programme. The best islands to try are Santiago, Brava, Santo Antão and São Nicolau. Snorkelling and turtle- and whale-watching are all likely to appeal to budding naturalists: the flat islands of Sal, Boa Vista and Maio are the best for these. Sal and Boa Vista are also windsurfing and kitesurfing central, with plenty of multilingual instructors on hand to help youngsters learn the ropes. Finally, a visit to Fogo is bound to go down well with young volcanologists – there are lava fields to examine, and shingle slopes to bound down.

Friendly donkey

Calendar of Events

January Dia da Nacionalidade e dos Heróis Nacionais (20 Jan): concerts held in Praia. Festa de São Vicente (22 Jan) on São Vicente.

February Carnival on Shrove Tuesday, with grand costume parades (all islands, but especially São Vicente and São Nicolau). Several days of post-parade music and dance in Mindelo and elsewhere. Cinzas, Ash Wednesday, with all-day feasting on Santiago.

March/April Sexta-Feira Santa, Good Friday, and Pascóa, Easter.

April Kriol Jazz Festival, Praia: three nights of concerts in the Pracinha da Escola Grande. Festa de São Jorge (23 Apr) on Santiago.

May Bandeira de São Filipe (1 May), with horse races on Fogo; Festa de São José (1 May) on Santiago. Santa Cruz (Holy Cross, 3 May) on all islands, but especially Maio. Festival de Gambôa, Praia da Gambôa, Praia: Cape Verde's biggest pop and rock festival, a two-night event featuring major stars from Cape Verde and the West African mainland.

June Tabanca (first Sunday), with costume parades on Santiago. Festa de Santo António (13 June), on Santo Antão. Festa de São João Baptista (24 June), a major festival on all islands, but especially Brava and Santo Antão, where there's a long pilgrimage and horse races.

July Dia de Santa Isabel (4 July) on Boa Vista. Santiago Maior (25 July) on Santiago.

August Festival Internacional de Música, Baía das Gatas, São Vicente: Cape Verde's (small-scale) answer to Glastonbury, with three days of concerts on the beach. Festival de Música de Praia de Cruz, two days of concerts on Boa Vista.

September Nossa Senhora da Luz (9 Sept) on São Vicente. Nossa Senhora das Dores (15 Sept) on Sal. Mindelact, theatrical festival, Mindelo. Festival de Música da Praia de Santa Maria: two days of Cape Verdean and West African music, Sal.

November International music and culture festival Sete Sóis e Sete Luas in Ribeira Grande on Santo Antão.

December São Nicolau (6 Dec) on São Nicolau. Natal (25 Dec) Christmas. Noite de São Silvestre (31 Dec), with fireworks and parties.

EATING OUT

Cape Verdeans generally prefer to entertain friends and family at home rather than eat out, but despite this, every reasonably sized town has at least a couple of places to eat, many doubling as bars and music venues. Every hotel and *pensão* also has its own eatery, ranging from simple dining rooms which offer a dish of the day from the owner's kitchen, to upmarket restaurants with extensive à la carte menus.

WHERE TO EAT

Praia, along with the tourist honeypot of Santa Maria on Sal and the emerging resort island of Boa Vista, are the most expensive places to eat, with Santa Maria boasting the biggest selection of restaurants covering the widest variety of cuisines. Both Sal and Boa Vista have a good number of Italian and Portuguese restaurants, and Praia, as you'd expect, has a few international-style places worth visiting. For quality and atmosphere, however, the most enjoyable restaurant and café scene is in Mindelo, which has an excellent range of local-style eateries with broad appeal.

Perhaps because Cape Verdeans like to take their mealtimes at a leisurely pace, fast food has yet to catch on, and street food is usually limited to popcorn, peanuts, biscuits and *pasteis*, small fried

Stewed serra and vegetables

fish pastries. For something quick but substantial, it's best to look for a bakery or café. Some petrol stations also have snack bars or food counters.

Cape Verdean hotels and *pensões* almost always include breakfast in their room rate. The least you can expect each morning is bread, butter, jam and coffee or tea, but some places push the boat out with extravagant spreads of *cachupa*, bacon, eggs, cheese, cold meat, cake, pastries and fruit.

For lunch and dinner, simple, local-style restaurants are generally excellent value and immaculately kept, though their menus tend to be rather limited – some don't have a written menu at all, but will advise you what's fresh that day. Green vegetables and salad can be particularly hard to find. It's usual for dishes to be prepared from scratch, so you may wish to place your order, then go away for an hour or so to

Fresh vegetables at the Mercado do Platô in Praia

run errands or relax before returning.

The pricier, tourist-oriented restaurants in Santa Maria and Boa Vista and the executive-oriented places in Praia have more varied menus; this doesn't always guarantee higher quality, but some are very good.

Most restaurants are open from around midday to 2.30pm and 6pm to 10.30pm, but not mid-afternoon. Bars may stay open until after midnight, which is when the

Grilled fish

clubs start warming up. Cape Verde's café scene is rather limited: there are only a few cafés in the main towns and resorts, and none in the villages.

WHAT TO EAT

Surrounded by waters teeming with tuna, wahoo, mackerel, octopus and squid, Cape Verde is an excellent place to enjoy fish and seafood. Other treats include tropical fruit, handmade goat's cheese and Portuguese-inspired desserts.

Fish

Traditional Cape Verdean cuisine is plain, simple peasant fare. By far the most common dish served in local restaurants is grilled fish, either filleted or whole, served with rice, chips, boiled vegetables, salad, or any combination of these. Elaborate sauces and spices are rarely used, nor are they needed, since local fish is invariably extremely fresh

Cachupa, the national dish

and flavoursome. Steaks cut from the larger fish such as *serra* (wahoo), *espada* (swordfish) and *atum* (tuna, of which you may see several species) are particularly tasty. Seafood such as prawns, moray eels, octopus, squid and conch appears in delicious soups, stews and risottos. Grilled local lobster is a superb though pricey delicacy. Other fish dishes tend to be far more reasonably priced than meat dishes.

Speciality Dishes

Cape Verde's signature dish, *cachupa*, is a slow-cooked, rustic stew made from dried corn kernels and beans along with a variety of other vegetables. It dates back to Cape Verde's early days as a transatlantic trading post, when the islanders first started growing vegetables from the Americas such as maize, beans and cassava (manioc). Everyone has their own recipe, but it's always hearty and extremely filling. An embellished version, *cachupa rica*, also includes fish, chicken, pork or sausage and is served when a special occasion demands as luxurious a variety of ingredients as the cook can afford.

Restaurants sometimes offer *cachupa* as their dish of the day; at other times, you have to place your order the day before, as the dish takes so long to prepare. Cooking *cachupa* slowly allows it to develop a rich flavour, which improves even further when the leftovers are reheated. Yesterday's stew fried up with onions is a favourite country breakfast.

Other traditional slow-cooked dishes include *feijoada*, Cape Verde's take on the bean casserole that's popular all over the Lusophone world from Brazil to Mozambique, and *djagasida*, a slightly spicy Creole stew of ground maize, rice, vegetables and salted meat.

Cheese, Fruit and Desserts

Cape Verdean desserts tend to be rather sweet and are mostly inspired by Portuguese favourites: you may come across *pasteis de nata* (flaky custard tarts), *pudim* (a custard dessert, similar to crème caramel) and *bolos* (cakes made

How to Make Cachupa Rica

500g meat and/or fish (e.g. tuna steak, chicken or pork pieces, chopped sausage, in any combination)

1kg mixed vegetables (e.g. sweet potato, pumpkin, cassava, onions, plantain, cabbage)

400g dried corn kernels

2 bay leaves

400g dried mixed beans

chicken stock cube

1 large onion

olive oil

2 ripe tomatoes

paprika, parsley and salt

1 clove garlic

Soak the corn and beans overnight in a large pot. Change the water, add the bay leaves, stock cube and two tablespoons of oil, and bring to the boil. Fry the onion, tomatoes and garlic in oil with paprika, add to the pot, and leave to simmer slowly. When the corn and beans are cooked, fry the meat or fish and add to the pot, followed by the vegetables. Leave to simmer again, making sure the sauce does not boil dry. Allow to stand before serving.

with honey or fruit). An interesting variation on *pudim* is *pudim de queijo*, made with soft cheese.

Locally grown tropical fruit such as bananas, papayas and coconuts are available all year round; others such as mangoes and melons are seasonal. Papayas, mangoes and quince are made into *doces*, firm jellies which may be served for breakfast or as a dessert, with local *queijo de cabra* (handmade goat's cheese) – a delicious combination.

WHAT TO DRINK

Cape Verde is very proud of its wine-making tradition. The two main brands of wine from Fogo – Chã, with its distinctive smoking volcano logo, and newcomer Sodade – are found in bars and restaurants all over the country at reasonable prices. The quality can vary, but a decent year, with plenty of rain,

Fresh Produce

Relaxing on the beach with a picnic and a couple of guitars is a favourite way for Cape Verdeans to spend a Sunday afternoon. If you would like to do the same, it's worth bearing in mind that while the fruit, vegetable and fish markets on some islands are simply stuffed with tempting produce, others have little to offer for most of the year. By far the best markets are in Praia and Assomada (on Santiago), and Mindelo (São Vicente). The market in São Filipe (Fogo), though smaller, is also good. In fishing ports, it's possible to buy fish straight out of the sea by negotiating a price with the fishermen on the spot, while in the highlands of Santo Antão travellers can buy goat's cheese direct from the makers. Cape Verde has very few supermarkets, but there are small grocery shops in most towns; some petrol stations also sell groceries. Village shops can be easy to miss – they look much like ordinary houses, except for a sign saying *Mercearia*.

brings out a complex flavour in both the *branco* (white), a fresh, fruity moscatel, and the *tinto* (red), made from touriga or *preta tradicional* – rich, dark Portuguese grapes. The Chã range also includes Passito, a beautifully golden dessert wine with a strong flavour of raisins. The 2014 volcanic eruption destroyed many of the vineyards around Chã das Caldeiras but efforts to restore wine production in

Wine tasting at the Chã co-operative on Fogo

the area are ongoing. Some restaurants also offer wine from Portugal and elsewhere in Europe.

The local beer, Strela, is a cheap but unremarkable lager. Bars also sell Sagres and SuperBock from Portugal, and sometimes Beck's or Heineken. Standard soft drinks and bottled water from Portugal are also available everywhere.

The drink that's most distinctively Cape Verdean, however, is *grogue*, a powerful sugar-cane hooch, the islands' answer to Brazilian *cachaça*. It's so popular that it's sold in every village – if there's no bar as such, the local shopkeeper is likely to be licensed to dish up shots from behind the counter. As a tipple, it offers more brute force than flavour, but it works well with muddled sugar and lime over ice as a caipirinha. Some distillers mix it with honey or fruit syrup; this concoction is called *pontche*. The traditional distilleries in Santo Antão and São Nicolau are generally considered the best, though the islands also have plenty of home-brew enthusiasts who claim their own *grogue di terra* beats anything you can buy in a bar. A slightly more sophisticated alternative is *aguardente*, a type of eau-de-vie made from twice-distilled wine.

Grogue

Cape Verde's secret weapon is thought to be named after grog, the rum-and-water tipple favoured by the British sailors who stopped over in the islands' 19th-century heyday.

Most cafés and restaurants serve excellent locally grown coffee, prepared in either the Italian or Portuguese way and presented as an espresso (*café expresso*, or simply *um café*), a cappuccino or a latte (*galão*). At breakfast time, however, filter coffee is often served up. Tea is served European-style – you're given a bag to dunk in hot water.

TO HELP YOU ORDER IN PORTUGUESE…

Do you have a table for four? **Tem uma mesa para quatro pessoas?**

I'd like the bill, please. **Queria a conta, por favor.**

a beer (small/large) **uma cerveja (pequena/grande)**	milk **leite**
	pepper **pimenta**
	salad **salada**
bread **pão**	salt **sal**
butter **manteiga**	a sandwich **um sandwíche**
cheese **queijo**	a soft drink or juice **um sumo**
chips **batatas fritas**	
a coffee **um café**	soup **sopa**
a dessert **uma sobremesa**	starter **entrada**
dish of the day **prato do dia**	sugar **açucar**
	tea **chá**
fish **peixe**	vegetables **legumes**
fruit **fruta**	still/fizzy water **água sem gaz/com gaz**
an ice cream **um gelado**	
main course **prato principal**	a bottle/glass of wine **uma garrafa/um copo de vinho**
meat **carne**	

… AND READ THE MENU (A EMENTA)

arroz rice

atum tuna

bafas seafood tapas

batatas potatoes

cachupa maize and
bean stew

carvala mackerel

coteletas de porco
pork chops

espada swordfish

espetadas kebabs

feijão bean

feijoada bean stew

frango grilhado grilled
chicken

gambas prawns

garoupa grouper

lagosta lobster

lulas squid

mariscos seafood

molho sauce

moreia frita fried eel

ovos eggs

polvo octopus

pudim de leite caramel
custard

serra guisada stewed
wahoo

tarte de coco coconut
sponge

Colourful restaurant in Calhau, São Vicente

PLACES TO EAT

The following options include restaurants and cafés in hotels, towns and villages across the country, with a bias towards places which have an authentic, local feel. They include international-style restaurants with à la carte menus; resort restaurants with a choice of local fish dishes and favourites such as pizza, pasta and grills; cafés serving drinks, ice cream and snacks; and local eateries which typically offer a set three-course menu based around whatever fish is freshest that day. Many places have multilingual staff, but in the simpler eateries, Creole and Portuguese may be the only languages spoken. The price codes below indicate the approximate cost per person, including IVA (sales tax), of a three course meal with water and house wine.

€€€ over 35 euros   **€€** 20–35 euros   **€** below 20 euros

SAL

Atlantis €€ *Praia de Santa Maria, Santa Maria, tel: 242 1879*. In a great location right on the sand, this large, French-owned pavilion is a relaxed beach bar by day and a smart-casual restaurant by night. Spacious, so good for groups, it has a warm atmosphere and tasty Cape Verdean and European-style cooking. As well as French and Portuguese wine, it serves a powerful sangria, laced with local *grogue*.

Benvass € *Rua Beleza, Espargos, tel: 241 3935*. This no-frills restaurant serves a large selection of tasty seafood, grilled meat and fish, and local Cape Verdean dishes. Live music at weekends.

Chez Pastis €€€ *Rua Amílcar Cabral 5, Santa Maria, tel: 984 3696*, www.chezpastis.it. Cosy and welcoming little restaurant in a narrow courtyard festooned with bougainvillea and fairy lights. It serves delicious pasta dishes including tagliatelle with home-smoked fish (the house speciality), along with Italian-style grills. Highly recommended, arguably the best restaurant on the island. Evenings only, 6.30–11pm.

Café Criolo €€ *Travessia Patrice Lumumba, Santa Maria, tel: 242 1774*. Rightly popular with both locals and tourists, this restaurant serves simple but good Creole fare, plus salads and snacks. Its streetside terrace is a great spot to catch the last rays of sunshine in the afternoon.

Farolin €€ *Hotel Odjo d'Água, Zona do Farolinho, Santa Maria, tel: 242 1414*, www.odjodagua-hotel.com. Gorgeously situated, with its balcony and terrace hanging right over the turquoise sea, this nautical-themed restaurant offers tempting fresh fish and seafood dishes, plus burgers, spaghetti and risotto. It's also good for *cachupa rica* or *feijoada*, which need to be ordered the day before. Local bands play here several nights a week.

Grog's €€ *Hortela de Baixo, Espargos, tel: 241 4380*. This restaurant, sports bar and grill serves good, reasonably priced local cuisine. The tuna carpaccio and grilled shrimps are worth a try. Live music on Saturday evenings.

Ocean Café Pub €€ *Rua 15 Agosto, Santa Maria, tel: 242 1895*, www.oceancafe.com. International cuisine including pasta dishes, cheeseburgers and fish and chips. Local and Italian wines available. Live music every night.

Les Palmiers €€€ *Hotel Morabeza, Rua 1 de Junho, Santa Maria, tel: 242 1020*, www.hotelmorabeza.com. With stylish white cane furniture and parasols laid out under pretty acacia trees, this terrace restaurant is a genuinely elegant place to enjoy good European-style fare. It's particularly atmospheric on evenings when there's a live band playing. The chic upstairs bar, La Tortue (Tue–Fri and Sun 7–10pm), serves knockout caipirinhas and global cuisine.

BOA VISTA

Blue Marlin €€ *Largo de Santa Isabel, Sal Rei, tel: 251 1099*. Located right on the main square in the centre of town, so very easy to find, this pleasant restaurant specialises in freshly caught fish and seafood.

Estoril €€ *Estoril Beach Resort, Johao Cristao, Sal Rei, tel: 251 1078.* Unusually for a resort restaurant, this colourful place always has Cape Verdean dishes such as *feijoada* (bean stew) and *caldo de peixe* (fish soup) on the menu, along with Italian favourites.

Grill Luar € *Off Avenida Amílcar Cabral, Sal Rei, tel: 251 1730.* This Cape Verdean grill, on the top floor of a building north of the main square, has fine views; at weekends it sometimes hosts live music nights.

Kanta Morna Café €€ *Migrante Guest House, Avenida Amílcar Cabral, Sal Rei, tel: 251 1143.* Decorated with old black-and-white photos and understated furniture, this is by far the coolest hangout on the island. The bar is expertly stocked, and dinner in the pretty, lantern-lit courtyard is an elegant, leisurely treat. You are served a European-style set menu prepared using fresh local ingredients, and the food is always beautifully presented. Advance booking is advisable.

Rosy € *Avenida Amílcar Cabral, Sal Rei, tel: 251 1242.* A simple place serving good, Creole-style fish and meat dishes. If you visit Boa Vista on a day-trip from Sal, you may well have lunch here.

Sodade de Nha Terra € *Rabil, tel: 251 1048.* This simple village restaurant has oilcloth tables and no menu; instead, customers tuck into big plates of whatever fish is freshest that day, perhaps grilled grouper with a salt crust or *serra* served with garlic sauce. Very friendly atmosphere.

MAIO

Bar Tropical €€ *Stadtstrand, Vila do Maio, tel: 255 1847.* Right on the beach, this relaxed bar offers simple but tasty fish dishes, a variety of snacks and home-made cakes. Enjoy a relaxing drink with ocean views.

Tutti Frutti € *Avenida Amílcar Cabral, Vila do Maio, tel: 255 1575.* A friendly pizzeria, run by one of the islands' many Italian expats, offering reliably tasty and filling fare.

SANTIAGO

Alex €€€ *Pestana Trópico Hotel, Prainha, Praia, tel: 261 4200.* One of the best restaurants in the country, this serves specialities from Cape Verde and Portugal and fine international-style meat and fish dishes. The atmosphere is smart but relaxed; in good weather there's an option of taking a table on the pool terrace. Breakfast, lunch and dinner daily.

Atlântico €€€ *Hotel Oásis Praiamar, Prainha, Praia, tel: 260 8440,* www.oasisatlantico.com. Good local, Portuguese and international cuisine in a pleasant hotel restaurant with tables outside and lovely ocean views. Breakfast, lunch and dinner daily.

Baía Verde €€ *Tarrafal, tel: 266 1128.* Breezy and informal, this tourist-friendly Cape Verdean place has tables set up on a shaded terrace overlooking Tarrafal's popular sandy beach.

Cybercafé Sofia € *Rua Serpa Pinto 31, Platô, Praia, tel: 261 4205.* On a corner of Pracinha da Escola Grande, this is the only place on the Platô with pavement café tables. Even if you don't need to check your email (there are internet terminals inside), it's a good spot to pause over breakfast, a drink or a light meal such as chicken curry or an omelette.

O Pescador €€€ *Praia, tel: 260 2130,* www.praiaguesthouse. com. Expensive but excellent restaurant at an elegant Portuguese-run guesthouse. The menu includes Portuguese and Cape Verdean dishes, including very appealing appetizers and fish. Good wine list.

Quinta da Montanha €€ *Rui Vaz, near São Domingos, tel: 268 5002.* Hungry locals make the pilgrimage from Praia to this country hotel for its Sunday lunchtime buffet; some make a weekend of it. On warm days, the large terrace is an enjoyable place to relax in the mountain air.

Quintal da Música €€ *Avenida Amílcar Cabral, Platô, Praia, tel: 261 1679.* Tucked away behind an inconspicuous entrance marked '5al da Música', Praia's famous 'music yard' has hosted many a luminary of the Cape Verdean music scene. It has bags of atmosphere, whether you're here for a drink, a meal (there's a good, varied menu) or just to soak up some live sounds. Bands play nightly except Sundays.

FOGO

Le Bistro € *Alto São Pedro, São Filipe, tel: 281 2518.* A firm favourite with São Filipe's European and American residents and visitors, this German-owned restaurant serves simple but tasty food such as spaghetti with tomato sauce or grilled *serra* with coconut, in the quiet surroundings of a period building, decorated in colourful, bohemian style.

Christine € *Vila de Igreja, Mosteiros, tel: 283 1045.* This small-town *pensão* produces huge plates of grilled fish or chicken with vegetables; as usual in this kind of place, it's best to order an hour or so in advance or be prepared to wait. There's a dining room and a roof terrace.

Fogo Lounge €€ *São Filipe, tel: 281 1066.* This chic, modern restaurant occupies the front yard of the Colonial House B&B, shaded by sail-shaped awnings. A mellow spot for a hearty brunch of eggs, sausage and pancakes, a light lunch of pasta or kebabs, or an after-dark caipirinha.

Pipi's € *São Filipe, tel: 281 4156.* An ideal place to sample some African dishes, Poulet Yassa is highly recommended. Be sure to try the local caipirinha. Open daily until late.

Tortuga €€ *Tortuga B&B, São Filipe, tel: 994 1512,* www.tortuga-fogo.eu. The fish here is as fresh as it comes as the owner buys it straight from the fishermen on the beach. The prepared dishes are just as delicious, and the service is attentive and friendly. The home-made jams, liqueurs and cheeses are also worth trying.

Tropical Club € *São Filipe, tel: 281 2161.* Hugely popular with Europeans, this atmospheric bar-restaurant has a cosy, palm-shaded courtyard, Creole cooking, good service, and live music at weekends.

Xaguate €€–€€€ *São Filipe, tel: 281 5000*, www.hotelxaguate. org. The restaurant at the Hotel Xaguate is São Filipe's upmarket dining option, with fine views across the ocean to Brava and access to the pool terrace. International-style cuisine.

BRAVA

Sol na Baia €€ *Fajã d'Água, tel: 285 2070*, www.sol-na-baia.e-monsite.com. The Cape Verdean artist who owns this attractive bayfront house spent many years in France, and his cooking shows plenty of French influences – you can expect delicious sauces with your fish and home-grown vegetables. You may also have the chance to sample *grogue* from his boutique distillery.

SÃO VICENTE

Chez Loutcha €€ *Rua do Côco, Mindelo, tel: 232 1636*. This well-run restaurant has a pleasantly traditional ambience and a huge menu including Portuguese, Italian and Senegalese classics, but the main reason to drop by is to enjoy some traditional music – there are live sessions at least twice a week.

Hamburg € *Calhau, tel: 283 0916*. This colourful little no-frills restaurant serves what is perhaps the best grilled grouper you'll find in Cape Verde; other choices include tuna, moray eel and octopus, all straight out of the sea. You can stroll to the beach to chill out while they rustle up your order.

Café Mindelo €–€€ *Rua Governador Calheiros 6, Casa Café Mindelo, Mindelo, tel: 231 8731*, www.casacafemindelo.com. On the ground floor of a lovingly restored historic building with seven guest rooms on the first and second floors, this is Mindelo's hippest hangout. Poets, musicians and urbane tourists pile in from breakfast until late, for everything from coffee and pastries to *bacalhau* (salt cod) and rice or quiche and salad.

O Cordel Restaurante €€ *Madeiralzinho, Mindelo, tel: 231 6402.* An attractive restaurant with excellent food and service. The fish and meat dishes here are delicious, especially the filet mignon.

La Pergola €–€€ *Alliance Française, Rua de Santo António, Mindelo, tel: 982 7675.* The courtyard café at Mindelo's French cultural centre is a little oasis in the centre of town. The lunchtime dish of the day is always excellent value, and there's decent wine, pastis and fruit liqueurs to enjoy. Closed after 3pm on Sat, and all day Sun.

Pica-Pau €–€€ *Rua de Santo António 42, Mindelo, tel: 232 8207.* Tiny, old-fashioned eatery, famous for its *arroz de marisco* (seafood risotto) and grilled lobster, both of which are better than any you'll find on Sal or Boa Vista, but half the price. The interior is decidedly eccentric, with many messages of appreciation taped to the walls.

Pont d'Agua €€€ *Avenida Marginal, Mindelo, tel: 231 0112.* With a classy, modern interior this restaurant is situated in a lovely location at the marina. The menu offers inventive takes on classic fish and seafood dishes.

Simpático €€ *Rua Sena Barcelos, Mindelo, tel: 910 3030,* www.simpaticocaboverde.com. A mellow spot in the heart of Mindelo's historic centre serving daily specials and à la carte dishes. This bistro and bar also serves as a small gallery with photographs and paintings by local artists displayed on the walls.

Sodade €€ *Rua Franz Fanon 38, Mindelo, tel: 231 3370,* www.residencialsodade.com. The rooftop restaurant of this *pensão* opens onto a very spacious roof terrace with panoramic views of Mindelo and the bay. It serves very decent food at reasonable prices, with professional staff and enough sense of occasion to make it a favourite spot for locals at weekends.

SANTO ANTÃO

Caleta €–€€ *Ponta do Sol, tel: 225 1561.* With splendid views of the harbour, this restaurant offers good value for money. The varied and original menu includes a tasty cachupa and the boat-shaped bar serves a variety of drinks.

Cantinha do Gato Preto € *Ponta do Sol, tel: 225 1526.* The Black Cat Cantina at Ponta do Sol's Eki Eko gallery shop is bright, airy and pleasant, with mellow African tunes on the stereo. The menu features salads, omelettes, *cachupa*, local goat's cheese and fresh coffee. Daily.

Pedracin Village €€ *Boca de Coruja, tel: 224 2020.* The restaurant at this stunningly situated rural hotel, high up among beautiful mountain scenery, has a menu featuring island-grown produce, much of it from the Pedracin's own gardens.

SÃO NICOLAU

Alice € *Rua de Praia, Tarrafal, tel: 236 1187.* With a couple of hours' notice, the staff at this homely guesthouse will happily rustle up a filling three-course supper of soup, grilled or stewed freshly caught fish, and fruit, at a rock-bottom price.

Casa Aquario Restaurant €€ *Alto Calheta, Tarrafal, tel: 236 1099,* www.casa-aquario.nl. This Dutch-run guesthouse and restaurant is part of a private development scheme providing training for local young people. Excellent Cape Verdean and international dishes are available every day, while Italian, French, Hungarian and other dishes can be cooked on request.

A–Z TRAVEL TIPS

A Summary of Practical Information

A

ACCOMMODATION (Alojamento)

Cape Verde has a fairly wide range of accommodation but no official grading system; tour operators apply their own ratings to the establishments they feature. Since tourism is developing at different rates within the archipelago, the options vary a great deal from island to island.

Types of accommodation. In total, there are around 220 places to stay, with by far the biggest concentration to be found in the resort town of Santa Maria on Sal. Here, the most popular choices are middle-market beach-and-pool hotels aimed at European families and other holidaymakers. Cape Verdean resort hotels are mostly of a similar standard to the mid-range places found in the Canary Islands or the Balearics, but all are low-rise (with no more than five storeys) and low-key (nightlife throughout Cape Verde tends to be fairly subdued and mainly hotel-based).

Sal also has an increasing number of self-catering apartments (*apartamentos*), and a few local-style guesthouses (either called *pensões*, singular *pensão*; *residenciais*, singular *residencial*; or *pousadas*), which tend to be great value. Typically run by locals who may not speak any languages apart from Creole and Portuguese, *pensões* and *residenciais* are ideal for those looking for a more authentic Cape Verdean experience than that provided by the more tourist-oriented hotels. While some of the very cheapest ones are old-fashioned, with rather basic furnishings and no hot water, most are spotlessly kept. All provide linen, soap and towels. The more upmarket ones offer en suite rooms with a television, fridge and air conditioning.

Boa Vista's selection of beach hotels and apartments is growing, and may in time rival Sal's. Santiago and São Vicente each has a couple of dozen urban hotels and guesthouses aimed at both business travellers and tourists, plus a few coastal places. Maio, Fogo and Santo Antão each has one international-style coastal hotel and several appealing guesthouses. Accommodation on Brava and São Nicolau is limited to guesthouses.

At present, Cape Verde has no top-end hotels to compare with the best places found in other destinations, but there are large, elaborately designed all-inclusive resorts on both Sal and Boa Vista, and new luxury hotels are planned. Boutique accommodation is also a rarity: Mindelo on São Vicente has several boutique guesthouses and Sal Rei on Boa Vista one. Eco-friendly practices such as recycling and renewable energy production have yet to gain much of a foothold, but some places (particularly the *pensões* and *residenciais*) make a point of offering their guests local produce wherever possible.

I'd like a single/twin/double room. **Queria um quarto simples/duplo/casal.**
with a shower/hot water/half-board **com chuveiro/agua quente/meia pensão**
How much is it per night? **Quanto é por noite?**

Pricing policies. Hotels charge per room, rather than per person, but for single occupancy of a double room there may be a discount of 15–40 percent. High season in the beach resorts on Sal and Boa Vista corresponds with the European summer holidays: it's advisable to book a few months in advance for a stay in late July or August, which is when prices are highest. Some hotels also charge a premium at Easter, Christmas and New Year. Elsewhere, seasonal price variations are less common. Mindelo (São Vicente) and Ribeira Brava (São Nicolau) are always packed for the carnival celebrations in the run-up to Ash Wednesday in February, but price hikes at this time are rare.
Bookings. While all hotels and guesthouses accept direct book-

ings by phone or email, only some of them have websites. The most straightforward way to book, particularly if you're planning an island-hopping trip, is through a specialist travel agent such as the UK-based companies listed below. All have good local knowledge – they should, for example, be able to steer you away from places where building work, a fact of life on several islands, may cause disturbance. They can also coordinate flights, transfers and tours.

Cape Verde Travel, tel: 01964 536191, www.capeverdetravel.com
The Cape Verde Experience, tel: 0845 330 2047, www.capeverde.co.uk
Archipelago Choice, tel: 01768 775672, www.capeverdechoice.com

AIRPORTS *(Aeroportos)*

Cape Verde currently has four international airports and three domestic ones. Most European holidaymakers fly direct to Sal; there are also direct flights to the airport on Boa Vista. Santiago is the main arrival point for scheduled flights from Lisbon, Providence, RI, Fortaleza and Dakar, while the airport on São Vicente handles arrivals from Lisbon, Paris and Amsterdam.

The international airports each have a single terminal; these handle both international and internal flights, and have all the facilities you would expect, including vehicle hire and excursion company offices. They don't have official tourist information desks, however: these are non-existent in Cape Verde.

The aerodromes on Maio, Fogo and São Nicolau only handle internal flights and are small and basic, with no currency exchange desks, ATMs or other facilities. The airstrips at Mosteiros (Fogo), Ponta do Sol (Santo Antão) and Fajã d'Água (Brava) are disused, but still appear on some maps.

Every airport has a taxi rank but no regular public bus service. In theory it's possible to travel by shared *aluguer* between Sal airport and Espargos or Santa Maria, and between Boa Vista airport and Sal

Rei, but these, like all *aluguers*, run irregularly. Most tour operators and many hotels can provide transfers, either for free or for no more than the cost of a taxi, if booked in advance.

The local aviation authority, Empresa Nacional de Aeroportos e Segurança Aérea, tel: 241 1468 or 241 1372, can provide further details on airport facilities.

Sal: Amílcar Cabral, Espargos (SID), tel: 241 1468, 18km (11 miles) north of Santa Maria (20 min by taxi; fare €8–12).

Santiago: Nelson Mandela, Praia (RAI), tel: 263 8700, 3km (2 miles) northeast of Praia (10 min by taxi; fare €5–7).

Boa Vista: Aristides Pereira, Rabil (BVC), tel: 251 9000, 5km (3 miles) southeast of Sal Rei (10 min by taxi; fare €5–7).

São Vicente: Cesária Évora, São Pedro (VXE), tel: 230 0602, 9km (5.5 miles) southwest of Mindelo (10 min by taxi; fare €8–10).

Maio: Vila do Maio (MMO), tel: 255 1108, 3km (2 miles) north of Vila do Maio/Porto Inglês (10 min by taxi; fare €5–6).

Fogo: São Filipe (SFL), tel: 281 2107, 3km (2 miles) southeast of São Filipe (10 min by taxi; fare €5–6).

São Nicolau: Preguiça (SNE), tel: 235 1313, 3km (2 miles) south of Vila de Ribeira Brava (10 min by taxi; fare €5–6).

B

BICYCLE RENTAL *(Aluguer de bicicletas)*

It's possible to hire a mountain bike on Sal, Boa Vista, São Vicente or Santo Antão as many hotels offer bicycle rentals; the average cost is €10 per 4 hours, or €15 per 8 hours. There are a number of off-road tracks on the islands to be explored and cycling is a great way to see the stunning scenery.

BUDGETING FOR YOUR TRIP

The archipelago is not cheap for visitors, largely because so much – from fuel for the desalination plants to basic commodities for the hotels and restaurants – needs to be imported. Costs are highest in Santa Maria on Sal. Elsewhere, accommodation, food and drink are similar in price to rural France, Spain or Portugal.

Getting there. A standard return flight to Cape Verde from the UK costs £550–650; special offers can sometimes bring the fare down to as little as £199. Internal flights cost €30–75 per leg.

Accommodation. If booking direct, one night's bed and breakfast accommodation for two people sharing an en suite room costs €30–50 in a *pensão* and €50–225 in a hotel. A room for one costs €20–150. Booking through a tour operator may reduce these prices.

Food and drink. At lunchtime, a *prato do dia* (dish of the day) typically costs €5–8, while a three-course evening meal with water and house wine or local beer costs around €15 in a simple country eatery, or €30–50 in a resort restaurant, with a premium for specialities such as lobster. In bars and restaurants, the cheapest wine costs around €3 per glass or €11 per bottle; local beer is €1–2 for a small bottle; spirits are €1.50–5 per shot, soft drinks are €1.20–2.50, an espresso is around €0.50 and water is €1.20–2 for a large bottle.

Activities. Windsurfing gear costs €40–65 per day to hire; lessons are €35–50 per hour. Land-based day tours by minibus typically cost €30–65 per person including lunch; small-group, bespoke trips by 4x4 cost up to €120 per person. Bus and *aluguer* fares between villages start at around €1.50 per person. Taxis start at €3–4 for a short hop, rising swiftly to €60–90 for a full day. Hiring a vehicle costs €50–95 per day, plus €1.50 per litre for fuel. Most museums have a token entry fee of around €1.

C

CAR HIRE *(Aluguer de carros)*

Car hire is only recommended for very confident drivers, as many roads, particularly in rural areas, are steep, narrow, bumpy and poorly signed. An alternative is to hire a taxi with a driver for the day (see page 133).

If you do decide to hire a car, Hertz (www.hertz.com) operate from the airports on Sal and Santiago, and in Santa Maria and Praia; their standard rates start at around €85 per day for a medium-sized car. Local firm, Alucar, is cheaper at €50–70. If you're planning to leave the tarmac, you will need a 4x4. Drivers must be at least 21 years old, and must leave credit card details as a deposit.

Sal: Alucar, tel: 251 1145, www.alucar.cv

Boa Vista: Alucar, tel: 251 1445, www.alucar.cv

Santiago: Alucar, tel: 261 4520, www.alucar.cv

São Vicente: Alucar, tel: 232 8764, www.alucar.cv

I'd like to rent a small car. **Queria alugar um carro pequeno.**

for one day/one week **por um dia/uma semana**

today/tomorrow **hoje/amanhã**

Fill it up, please. **Encha, por favor.**

Are we on the right road for...? **É esta estrada para...?**

My car has broken down. **O meu carro está avariado.**

CLIMATE

Cape Verde is rightly promoted as a year-round holiday destination; compared to other tropical countries, the climate is moderate, though arid and windy.

Climatic conditions vary considerably from island to island: it rarely rains on Sal, Boa Vista or São Vicente, while the mountains of Santo Antão and Santiago receive enough rain and cloud to keep them green all year round.

The annual averages disguise a variety of extremes. In general, the long, dry season (Nov–June) brings warm, sunny days, but nights can be chilly, particularly in the mountains or when the north-easterly winds are most severe (Jan–Mar). The windiest days are excellent for watersports, but disappointing for sunbathers. Temperatures rise in the humid season (July–Oct), when the luckier islands receive occasional rain storms. It can be extremely hot on Sal, Boa Vista and Maio in late summer (Aug–Oct).

Average daytime temperatures:

	J	F	M	A	M	J	J	A	S	O	N	D
°C	23	22	21	22	23	25	25	26	27	27	26	24
°F	73	72	70	72	73	77	77	79	81	81	79	75

CLOTHING

Most Cape Verdeans are open-minded Christians who dress in Western style; tidy but casual is the norm at all times of day. If you're visiting in winter, or dividing your time between the beach and the mountains, you will need warm layers as well as hot-weather clothing. You should bring shoes or sandals which are comfortable enough to cope with cobbled streets; hikers will also need boots or shoes with ankle support.

If you're island-hopping, limiting yourself to hand luggage will save a lot of time. Washing and drying clothes, or getting them laundered, is straightforward.

CRIME AND SAFETY

Most visits to Cape Verde are trouble-free, but it's important to take common-sense precautions against petty crime such as bag-snatching in Santa Maria, Praia and Mindelo, and on beaches. Walking alone at night is not recommended.

If you're a victim of crime, you should report it, even if you have little hope of redress. A photocopy of your passport ID page, tickets and credit cards will help speed up the process of making a police report in the event of their loss.

D

DRIVING

Driving is only recommended for very confident drivers. Although some roads are very good, many are difficult to drive on, steep, narrow, bumpy and poorly signed. However, traffic is generally light: you may find yourself giving lifts to a succession of pedestrians.

Vehicles drive on the right, seat belts are compulsory and the speed limits are 50kmh (31mph) in towns and 90kmh (56mph) on other roads. Fuel is available at stations in every main town on the islands.

There is no national breakdown service. Seek advice from your car hire company about what to do in case of an accident.

E

ELECTRICITY

Electrical current in Cape Verde is 220V, 50Hz. European-style sockets and plugs with two round pins are standard.

> I need an adaptor/a battery. **Preciso de um adaptador/ uma pilha.**

EMBASSIES AND CONSULATES (Embaixadas e Consulados)

US: Rua Abilio Macedo 6, Praia, Santiago, tel: 260 8900, http://praia. usembassy.gov.

Britain, Ireland, Canada, South Africa, Australia and New Zealand do not have embassies in Cape Verde. The British Honorary Consul in Mindelo, Antonio Canuto (tel: 232 2830), or his assistant Isabel Spencer (tel: 232 3512), can help with consular emergencies only. The closest British embassy is in Dakar, Senegal (tel: +221 33 823 7392, http://ukinsenegal.fco.gov.uk).

EMERGENCIES *(Emergências)*

Police *(Polícia)* 132
Fire *(Bombeiros)* 131
Ambulance *(Ambulância)* 130

G

GAY AND LESBIAN TRAVELLERS

Cape Verdeans favour equal opportunities for individuals of any gender, sexuality or race, and the age of consent is the same for all, 16 years. Nonetheless, attitudes tend to be fairly conservative, and there is no overt gay scene. In 2013 Mindelo on São Vicente hosted Cape Verde's first gay pride week.

GETTING THERE

Travellers from the UK can reach Cape Verde by direct charter flight to Sal or Boa Vista from Gatwick, Birmingham or Manchester with Thomson (http://flights.thomson.co.uk; 6hrs) or scheduled flight to Santiago, Sal, Maio, São Vicente or São Nicolau islands via Lisbon with TAP Portugal (www.flytap.com; 10hrs+). There are also direct flights to Sal and Boa Vista from several other cities in Europe.

There is one direct route from the US, from Providence, RI to Santiago with TACV (www.flytacv.com; 9hrs). Other direct routes to Cape Verde include TACV from Dakar and Fortaleza; Air Sénégal International from Dakar; and TAAG Angola from São Tomé and Luanda.

GUIDES AND TOURS *(Guias e Excursões)*

Since tourism is still in its infancy, the quality of tours available is rather variable, and some are overpriced, but all the following are recommended; they offer well-planned trips with English-speaking (or multilingual) guides.
Sal: Barracuda Tours, Edifício Barracuda, Zona Praia 33, Santa

Maria, tel: 242 2033, www.barracudatours.com; Morabitur, Oásis Plaza Building, Santa Maria, tel: 242 2070 or (airport) 241 2672, www.morabitur.com.

Boa Vista: Barracuda Tours, Avenida 4 de Julho 236C, Sal Rei, tel: 251 1907, www.barracudatours.com; Morena, tel: 251 1445, www.boavistamorena.com.

Santiago: Tour De World Agency, Avenida Cidade de Lisboa, Praia, tel: 262 3078, www.tourdeworldagency.weebly.com.

Fogo: Qualitur, Praça 4 de Setembro, São Filipe, tel: 281 1089, www.qualitur.cv.

São Vicente: Barracuda Tours, Rua de Coco 28A, Mindelo, tel: 232 5591, www.barracudatours.com; Sabura Adventures, Rua Angola 61A, Mindelo, tel: 977 5681, www.sabura-adventures.com.

Brava: Qualitur, Edifício Áqua Brava, Nova Sintra, tel: 285 2867, www.qualitur.cv.

H

HEALTH AND MEDICAL CARE

Compared to many tropical countries, Cape Verde presents few health risks to visitors. The main dangers are dehydration and sunburn, even on cloudy and windless days. Malaria is practically absent, with just occasional occurrences on Santiago between September and November; visitors should protect themselves against mosquitoes at this time, but are unlikely to be prescribed a course of prophylactics. Although at present there is no risk of yellow fever in this country, a vaccination certificate is required for travellers arriving from a yellow-fever-affected area. Other recommended vaccinations include typhoid, hepatitis A and B and tetanus/diphtheria/polio.

Nonetheless, all visitors should have travel insurance including emergency cover, as medical facilities in the islands are limited. All serious cases must be flown to the major hospitals on Santiago (Hospital de Doctor Agistinho Neto, Largo Martires de Pidjiguiti, Plato, Praia, tel: 260 2140), Sal (Hospital do Sal, Bairro Novo, Espargos, tel. 241 1130) or São Vicente (Hospital de Doctor Baptista de Sousa, Mindelo, tel: 232 7355), or repatriated.

All the islands have clinics and pharmacies (*farmácia*; open during normal shopping hours) which are equipped to deal with most minor complaints.

Much of Cape Verde's tap water comes from desalination plants or storage tanks: islanders drink it without any ill effects but visitors are advised to purify it or stick to bottled water, which is cheap to buy from local shops. Food hygiene is generally good, particularly in small restaurants which use fresh, rather than frozen, produce. However, it's advisable to avoid eating raw vegetables.

I need a doctor/dentist. **Preciso de um médico/ dentista.**

upset stomach **dôr de estômago**

sunburn/fever **queimadura de sol/febre**

L

LANGUAGE

Most Cape Verdeans are bilingual in Portuguese (the official language) and Creole (the preferred language, derived from a blend of Portuguese, African languages and English). In tourist hotels, receptionists and waiters may also speak English, French, Italian or German. Elsewhere, French and English are fairly widely spoken, thanks to the influence of Francophone West Africa, the islanders' many American connections and the growth of tourism.

The language box below has some useful words and phrases in Portuguese and Creole. The other language tips given in this chapter are in Portuguese.

English **Portuguese** Creole

hello/hi **olá/tchau** ola/oi

good morning **bom dia** bon dia

good afternoon **boa tarde** bo tard

good evening **boa noite** bo not

How are things? **Tudo bem?** Tud dret?

Fine, thanks. **Tudo bem, obrigado**. Tud dret obrigadu.

I'm sorry, I don't understand. **Desculpe, não compreendo**.
   Disculpam, n ka ta konprende.

Do you speak English/French/Portuguese? **Fala inglês/
   francês/português?** Bu tu papia ingles/frances/portuges?

How much is it? **Quanto custa?** Es e tont?

please **por favour** pur favor

May I...? **Posso...?** N podi...?

Can you...? **Pode...?** Bu podi...?

yes/no **sim/não** sin/nau

You're welcome. **Não tem de quê/De nada.** Es é ka nada/
   Di nada.

goodbye **tchau** tchau

See you later. **Até logo.** Te logu.

M

MAPS (Mapas)

The speed at which Cape Verde is developing means that maps
date quickly. Among the more useful ones is the rip-proof Reise
Know-How 1:135,000 Cabo Verde map. Goldstadt-Verlag's Wan-
derkarte series of six 1:50,000 or 1:60,000 island maps (Boa Vista/
Sal/Maio; Santiago; Fogo/Brava; São Vicente; Santo Antão; São
Nicolau) are useful for detailed exploration, with GPS references
and routes for hikers. They are sometimes sold in Cape Verdean
shops and hotels. Cape Verde has no official distributor of free

tourist maps; the only ones available are the rough town plans offered by some hotels.

MEDIA

Newspapers. Cape Verde's most-read newspaper is *A Semana*, a Portuguese-language weekly with an online version in English (www.asemana.publ.cv). The newsagent at Sal airport stocks a few English-language magazines; newspapers from the UK are not normally available.

Radio. The state radio network, Rádio de Cabo Verde (RCV), broadcasts on frequencies which vary from island to island, along with international services such as RDP África (in Portuguese), BBC World Service and Voice of America (in English) and RFI Afrique (in French). Local music stations include Crioula FM (94.9) and Praia FM (94.1).

TV. The state-owned broadcaster, Radio e Televisão Caboverdiana (RTC), runs one television channel, Televisão de Cabo Verde (TCV), showing programmes in Portuguese and Creole, including live sport and hugely popular Brazilian *telenovelas* (soaps). Hotel televisions are also usually tuned to RTP Africa (in Portuguese), CNN (in English) and Canal Plus (in French).

MONEY (Dinheiro)

The local currency is the escudo (CVE), which is pegged to the euro at a fixed exchange rate of approximately €1:CVE110. There are 200, 500, 1,000, 2,000 and 5,000 escudo notes, and 1, 5, 10, 20, 50 and 100 escudo coins.

Escudos are not available outside Cape Verde but can be obtained at the fixed rate on the islands from ATMs (fast and convenient, but pricey if your bank's transaction charges are high), airport forex bureaux or banks (found in every town, but sometimes rather slow). It's expensive to change escudos back into euros or pounds.

Many tourist-oriented businesses accept euros, Visa and Master-

Card or travellers' cheques, although most make a surcharge for this, either by adjusting the exchange rate or adding a fee, typically 5–6 percent for euro notes, Visa or MasterCard, and 10 percent for travellers cheques' or euro coins (a €1 coin is taken as having a value of CVE100). UK pounds and US dollars are straightforward to exchange but are not normally accepted as payment.

Prices in escudos are often written with a dollar sign in place of a decimal point: 200$00 means the same as CVE200. Large amounts are sometimes expressed in 'contos', conto being an old expression for a thousand escudos; thus quinhentos contos (500 contos) means CVE500,000.

While most hotels, restaurants and shops include IVA (sales tax) in their quoted prices, a few add it separately: the rate is 6 percent for hotel and restaurant bills and 15 percent for other goods and services.

How much is that? **Quanto custa isto?**
Can I pay by credit card? **Posso pagar com cartão de crédito?**
I want to change some pounds/euros. **Queria cambiar libras/euros.**
Where's the nearest bank? **Onde fica o banco mais próximo?**
Is there an ATM here? **Há uma caixa aqui?**

OPENING TIMES *(Horários)*

Most Cape Verdeans work a five-day week, with a break for lunch. **Banks** are open Mon–Fri 8am–3pm. **Shopping** hours are typically Mon–Fri 8am–noon and 3–7pm, Sat 9am–1pm; souvenir shops and convenience stores sometimes have longer hours. **Petrol stations** are usually open all day, until 10.30pm.

On Sundays, most restaurants, bars and petrol stations are open, but almost everything else is closed. Churches are generally only open for services.

> open/closed **aberto/cerrado**
> What time does it open/close/start/finish? **A que horas abre/fecha/comença/acaba?**

P

POLICE

In an emergency, call 132. Phone numbers for the main police station (*posto de polícia*) on each island are:

Sal, tel: 241 1132
Santiago, tel: 262 1232
Boa Vista, tel: 251 1132
São Vicente, tel: 231 4631
Maio, tel: 255 1132
Santo Antão, tel: 222 1132
Fogo, tel: 281 1132
São Nicolau, tel: 235 1132
Brava, tel: 285 1132

> I want to report a theft. **Quero participar un furto.**
> My wallet has been stolen. **A minha carteira foi roubada.**
> I've lost my bag/passport. **Perdi o meu saco/passaporte.**

POST OFFICES (*Correios*)

Every major town has a post office, typically open Mon–Fri 8am–noon and 2.30–5pm; some double as stationery and phone shops.

Many hotels sell stamps and take items to the post office (there are no post boxes in Cape Verde). The rate for an international card or letter is CVE60.

PUBLIC HOLIDAYS *(Feriados)*

1 Jan *Ano Novo* New Year's Day
13 Jan *Dia da Democracia* Democracy Day
20 Jan *Dia dos Heróis Nacionais* National Heroes' Day
Feb, varies *Terça-Feira de Carnaval* Shrove Tuesday
Mar/Apr, varies *Sexta-Feira Santa* Good Friday
Mar/Apr, varies *Páscoa* Easter Sunday
1 May *Dia do Trabalhador* Labour Day
1 June *Dia Internacional da Criança* Children's Day
5 July *Dia da Independência* Independence Day
15 Aug *Dia da Assunção de Nossa Senhora da Graça* Feast of the Assumption
1 Nov *Dia de Todos os Santos* All Saints' Day
25 Dec *Natal* Christmas

T

TELEPHONES

To call a Cape Verdean number from abroad or from a non-Cape Verdean mobile, dial +238 followed by the seven-digit number. From a Cape Verdean landline or mobile, you can call any of the islands by just dialling the seven-digit number.

To make an international call from a Cape Verdean phone, dial 00, the country code and the number (omitting any initial zero).

Low-cost phone calls. If there's a phone in your hotel room, it's wise to ask about call charges before using it – they may be extortionate. Internet phone services such as Skype are far cheaper, particularly for international calls. Cheap calls can also be made in post offices and town-centre telecentres; having completed your call, you pay at the counter.

A convenient, though pricier, alternative is to buy a TeleFácil phonecard, priced from CVE200; the credit can be used to call from any private or public phone (public phones don't take coins). Phonecards are sold at general stores and CV Telecom shops, which are found in the international airports and main towns.

Mobile phones. Most UK mobile phones will work in Cape Verde, but you should check with your service provider and be prepared for high charges for both making and receiving calls and sending text messages.

The most economical way to stay in mobile contact with your travel companions (and anybody else in Cape Verde) is to buy a local prepaid (*pré-pago*) SIM card. Available from CV Telecom and mobile phone shops, these include free voicemail and work with any unlocked mobile (unlock codes for most phones can be obtained online).

Currently, CV Telecom's CVMóvel network, www.cvmovel.cv, has the best mobile coverage across the country; their SIM cards are cheap (from CVE200) and top-up cards (*cupão de recargo*) start at CVE300. The Unitel T+ network (www.unitelmais.cv) is also quite extensive.

TIME ZONE

Cape Verde stays on GMT -1 all year round. The chart below shows the time differences Cape Verde and various cities in winter. In summer, when clocks are put forward an hour in the UK and US the time difference changes by an hour.

New York	**Cape Verde**	London	Jo'burg	Sydney	Auckland
8am	**noon**	1pm	3pm	midnight	2am

TIPPING

Cape Verde has no formal culture of tipping and service charges. It's up to the individual to decide whether to leave a token of appreciation for hotel and restaurant staff but a small tip is always welcome

TOILETS *(Casas de banho)*

Public toilets are rare in Cape Verde, but those in bars and restaurants are generally of a good standard.

Where is the toilet? **Onde é a casa de banho?**

TOURIST INFORMATION

Cape Verde has no official tourist information organisation; the best people to approach for advice before you leave are the specialist travel agents listed on page 109.

TRANSPORT

Local transport services appear and disappear on a regular basis. The following are all in operation at the time of writing.

Internal flights. Scheduled flights connect all the islands except Brava, Santo Antão and Santa Luzia. The hubs are Sal (for Boa Vista, Santiago, Fogo, São Vicente and São Nicolau) and Santiago (for Sal, Boa Vista, Maio, Fogo and São Vicente). There are also direct flights between São Vicente and São Nicolau. Flights between Sal, Santiago, Boa Vista and São Vicente leave daily; others run between three and six times a week. All flights take under 50 minutes; Santiago to Maio is the shortest at under 15 minutes. Check-in begins an hour before take-off.

The national airline, TACV (www.flytacv.com), is the main operator. The service used to be plagued by delays but seems to have improved recently. Empty seats are rare, so it's best to book well in advance: their UK agent is The Cape Verde Experience (tel: 0845 330 2047, www.capeverde.co.uk). In Cape Verde, reservations can be made by email (reservas@tacv.aero) or through their island offices: Sal, tel: 241 1338; Boa Vista, tel: 251 1186; Santiago, tel: 260 8274;

Fogo, tel: 281 1228; São Vicente, tel: 232 6712; São Nicolau, tel: 235 1161, and Santo Antão, tel: 221 1184.

Ferries. There are ferry connections to all major inhabited islands. Fares are very reasonable, though many operators have no regular schedules, and even if they do, delays are common. It's always best to ask for information on site. Tickets are sold at harbours and can be booked in advance only with Fast Ferry (tel: 261 7552, www.cvfast ferry.com).

Fast Ferry offers daily connections between Mindelo (São Vicente) and Porto Novo (Santo Antão); the *Liberdadi* catamaran journey takes around half an hour. *Liberdadi* also plies the São Vicente-São Nicolau route twice a weeks, a journey of 2 hours, 45 minutes. Another Fast Ferry catamaran, *Kriola*, links the Fogo and Brava islands five times a week (40 minutes). Fast Ferry also offers several other connections, including Brava-Santiago, and Fogo-Santiago several times a week.

Naviera Armas' *Mar D'Canal* runs a daily service between Mindelo (São Vicente) and Porto Novo (Santo Antão), taking around 60 minutes.

Another shipping company, Polar Agency, offers connections between the Fogo and Santiago islands three times a week on board the *Sotavento*.

Taxis. Unlike elsewhere in West Africa, most Cape Verdean taxis are new and well maintained. They're easily recognised by their livery (blue with a yellow stripe on Sal, cream on Santiago, yellow on Fogo, white with a checked stripe on São Vicente, blue on Santo Antão) and illuminated sign. Short hops may be metered but longer trips and full days are charged at a flat rate which is set by the local government. Tips aren't expected.

Where can I get a taxi? **Onde posso encontrar um táxi?**
How much will it cost to central Praia? **Quanto vai custar ao centro de Praia?**

Does this minibus go to Cidade Velha? **Vai para Cidade Velha este Hiace?**
How much is it to Santa Maria? **Quanto é para Santa Maria?**
Could you tell me when to get off? **Pode dizer-me quando devo sair?**

City buses. Praia and Mindelo have efficient urban and suburban transport networks; the buses indicate their destination, and stops are marked *Paragem*. You pay the driver as you board.

Shared taxis. Privately owned licensed minibuses or pick-up trucks with benches in the back, called *aluguers* or *Hiaces* (pronounced 'yass'), operate like buses, but with no timetable and no fixed stops – the driver decides when to leave and picks up or drops off on request. Recognisable by their sign saying *Aluguer* (for hire), they generally follow a standard route but will often make diversions if asked.

Fares are fixed; you pay the driver as you get off. It's also possible to hire an *aluguer* as a private taxi; this costs around 10 times the shared-taxi (*coletivo*) fare.

TRAVELLERS WITH DISABILITIES

Facilities for disabled travellers visiting Cape Verde are very limited: for advice, consult a specialist travel agent (see page 117).

V

VISAS AND ENTRY REQUIREMENTS

All non-Cape Verdean visitors require a full passport valid for at least six months beyond their intended return date, and an entry visa, which can be obtained in advance or on arrival. Tour operators and airlines will arrange single-entry tourist visas (€25) on request: you should send them a photocopy or scan of your passport ID page at least a week before departure so they can forward this to the island authorities, who will stamp the visa in your passport when you arrive.

If you have booked your trip at short notice, you can obtain a visa at passport control on arrival, although this can take up to two hours to complete.

There's no Cape Verdean consulate in the UK; the nearest is in Brussels (Ambassade du Cap-Vert, Avenue Jeanne 29, 1000 Bruxelles, tel: +32 2 64 69 025, email: emb.caboverde@skynet.be). The Cape Verde embassy in Dakar, Senegal, also issues visas.

W

WEBSITES AND INTERNET ACCESS

www.asemana.publ.cv Website of the popular newspaper *A Semana* with local news in Portuguese, English and French.

www.bela-vista.net Tourist information, including useful accommodation listings and ferry timetables.

www.capeverdeportal.com Information about Cape Verde islands, plus maps and a guide to interesting activities.

www.viajaracaboverde.com Information on hotels and places to go in Cape Verde.

www.caboverde24.com Commercial portal with links to many relevant sites.

www.cabocontact.com The website of the tourist information office in Mindelo.

www.governo.cv Official site of the Cape Verdean government.

Internet access. Free Wi-fi is provided in a growing number of public locations including the airports on Sal, São Vicente and Santiago, the main squares of many towns and many hotels. Data transfer limits vary. Some public libraries, such as the Mediateca in Mindelo, have terminals which are free to use. Every town also has at least one telecentre with fast and reasonably priced terminals (typically around €2 per hour).

Recommended Hotels

The following recommendations include hotels, *residenciais*, *pensões* and *pousadas*, with a bias towards places with a warm, authentic atmosphere. All but two of the options listed offer en suite facilities with hot water; it's also possible to find simpler places with shared bathrooms and/or cold water only. Almost all of the recommended establishments have a restaurant or dining room which is open to non-residents; those which serve particularly good food are described in more detail under Recommended Restaurants (see page 119).

The price codes indicate the approximate rate per night for two people sharing a room in high season, including breakfast and IVA (sales tax). A supplement may apply at peak times such as Christmas and Easter. For further information, see page 115.

€€€€	over 140 euros
€€€	80–140 euros
€€	40–80 euros
€	below 40 euros

SAL

Les Alizés €€ *Rua 1 de Junho, Santa Maria, tel: 242 1446*, www.hotel-les-alizes-cape-verde.com. In an attractively restored *sobrado* with a first-floor veranda and a roof terrace (great for breakfast on warm mornings), this cosy *pensão* has 10 simple but pleasant rooms, but no pool.

Dunas de Sal €€€ *Ponta Preta, Santa Maria, tel: 242 9050*, www.hoteldunasdesal.com. Moderately sized and stylish, with sleek, modern decor, this place isn't right on the beach but has a pool that's attractive enough to compensate.

Morabeza €€€€ *Rua 1 de Junho, Santa Maria, tel: 242 1020*, www.hotelmorabeza.com. A perennial favourite, rising graciously above its rapidly changing surroundings. Attractive and central, the Morabeza is almost everything a resort hotel should be; the food is good, there's a varied programme of things to do including local-interest activities such as *oril* and Creole lessons, and the highly professional, multilingual staff have just the right touch.

Nha Terra €€ *Rua 1 de Junho, Santa Maria, tel: 242 1109, email:* nha terra@hotmail.com. Right in the middle of town, this *pensão* has the feel of a well-kept budget hotel, with modest but sunny rooms plus a small swimming pool.

Oásis Atlantico Salinas Sea Resort €€€€ *Santa Maria, tel: 242 2300,* www.oasisatlantico.com. With a spa, swimming pool, fitness centre and several good restaurants, this 337-room resort hotel is located on the sands of Santa Maria's lovely white beach.

Odjo d'Água €€€ *Zona do Farolinho, Santa Maria, tel: 242 1414,* www.odjodagua-hotel.com. With around 100 rooms sharing the tiniest of swimming pools, this hotel can feel a little cramped, but it's right on an attractive beach, the restaurant is good and there's a pleasant, homely atmosphere.

Hotel Riu Garopa/Funana €€€€ *Cabocan, Santa Maria, tel: 242 9060, 242 9040,* www.riu.com. With 1,000 rooms in two beachfront hotel buildings and ten-odd bungalows, this is the biggest hotel complex on Sal. This five-star all-inclusive establishment has four excellent theme restaurants and offers entertainment programmes for children and adults.

BOA VISTA

Estoril Beach Resort €€€ *Sal Rei, tel: 251 1078, email:* info.estoril boavista@gmail.com. This pleasant and unpretentious Italian-run 3-star hotel has simple, colourful rooms and is within easy walking distance of the town centre. There's no pool, but Sal Rei's busiest windsurfing bases are nearby. The restaurant specialises in Italian and local cuisine, with live traditional music once a week.

Iberostar Club Boa Vista €€€€ *Praia de Chaves, Sal Rei, tel: 251 2170,* www.iberostar.com. This all-inclusive five-star hotel overlooks one of the loveliest beaches of the archipelago. Its 276 well-equipped, sunny rooms are spread across 17 buildings on a small hill. Mini- and maxi-clubs for children, and a clean, sandy beach make the hotel ideal for families.

Migrante €€€ *Avenida Amílcar Cabral, Sal Rei, tel: 251 1143*, www. migrante-guesthouse.com. Cool enough to catch the eye of style writers, this guesthouse has the feel of a riad. Around its beautifully restored courtyard are just four rooms, decorated with African fabrics and gauzy drapes; one is named after the Moroccan family who built the house in the 19th century, and the others after explorers.

Parque das Dunas €€€ *Praia de Chaves, tel: 251 1290*, www.parque dasdunas.com. A relaxed, simply-furnished 3-star hotel with an un- beatable location – its pool terrace and many rooms open straight onto the long, lovely beach.

Spinguera €€€€ *Espinguera, tel: 251 1941*, www.spinguera.com. With a pared-down, desert-island quality, this is an eco-retreat for escapists who are happy to do without television or a mobile phone signal. Cre- ated by an Italian artist on the site of an abandoned fishing village on a wild and isolated stretch of the northern coast, its stone cottages blend beautifully with the environment, and use renewable energy.

MAIO

Bela Vista €€ *Praia de Morro, tel: 256 1388*. Quiet, open-plan hotel, with spacious accommodation in 22 two-bedroom bungalows on a breezy beach.

Pensaò Big Game Maio € *Amílcar Cabral, Vila do Maio, tel: 971 0593*, www.biggamemaio.com. This small-scale ten-room *pensão*, with a restaurant, quad bike rental and a fishing centre, is a reliable choice for budget travellers. Welcoming, sea-themed rooms.

SANTIAGO

Oásis Atlantico Praiamar €€€€ *Prainha, Praia, tel: 260 8440*, www.oasisatlantico.com. Located in Praia's embassy district, this large, 123-room Portuguese chain hotel includes four suites, plus all the facilities you would expect of an upmarket establishment: a restaurant, bar, swimming pool, jacuzzi, sauna, gym and tennis court. It also offers romantic views of the rocky coastline.

Pestana Trópico €€€ *Prainha, Praia, tel: 261 4200,* www.pestana. com. Aimed at both tourists and business travellers, this is one of Santiago's more upmarket hotels, with courteous staff, a good-sized pool and a renowned restaurant.

Pôr do Sol €€ *Cidade Velha, tel: 267 1622.* Small, pleasantly untouristy hotel in a quiet coastal location, with a pool seemingly hanging right over the sea. The centre of Cidade Velha is within walking distance.

Praia Maria €€ *Rua 5 de Julho, Platô, Praia, tel: 261 8580, email:* res.praia maria@cvtelecom.cv. This smart little *residencial* is equipped with plain but modern furnishings and is located right in the centre of the capital.

Quinta da Montanha €€ *Rui Vaz, near São Domingos, tel: 268 5002, email:* quintamontanha@cvtelecom.cv. Close to challenging hiking trails among craggy peaks and ridges, this 28-room rural hotel has a friendly, family atmosphere, fantastic views of the surrounding mountain scenery and a telescope through which to enjoy the clear night sky.

Tarrafal €€ *Tarrafal, tel: 266 1785.* This small, plainly-furnished coastal hotel has 12 rooms, a buffet restaurant, snack bar and fitness centre.

FOGO

Bela Vista € *Achada Pato, São Filipe, tel: 281 1734.* Very central, this efficiently-run, spotless *pousada* has a pleasantly old-fashioned atmosphere and is excellent value.

Colonial House €€ *São Filipe, tel: 991 4566,* www.thecolonialguest house.com. From the balconies of this painstakingly restored 1883 *sobrado* house-turned B&B you can enjoy glimpses of the neighbouring Brava island. The Fogo Lounge restaurant (see page 110) is located in the front yard of the hotel.

Savana €€ *Alto São Pedro, São Filipe, tel: 281 1490,* www.hotelsavana fogo.com. In a restored *sobrado* on a quiet street uphill from the market, this 16-room hotel has a calm atmosphere. Several rooms are very grandly proportioned and elegant, and there's the bonus of a tiny pool. There's a good restaurant, Le Bistro, next door.

Xaguate €€€ *São Filipe, tel: 281 5000,* www.hotelxaguate.com. The best of the 38 well-furnished rooms at this São Filipe's top address have lovely ocean views. Breakfast is excellent, and the pool is the only good one in town.

BRAVA

Hotel Paraizo € *Cova Rodela de Cima, Vila Nova Sintra, tel: 285 2646.* This small hotel offers simple rooms with shared bathrooms. Balconies are great for contemplating beautiful mountain views.

Sol na Baia €€ *Fajã d'Água, tel: 285 2070,* www.sol-na-baia.e-mon site.com. With inspiring sea views, bedrooms flooded with sunlight, interesting oddments scattered around and a fantastic garden, this small three-room *pensão* really has an artist's touch of the owner, a local painter who's also a fine cook.

SÃO VICENTE

Casa Mindelo €€ *Rua Governador Calheiros 6, Mindelo, tel: 231 8731,* www.casacafemindelo.com. Bohemian, with just seven bedrooms and shared bathrooms, this is easily the most stylish place to stay in Mindelo. In the same lovingly restored late 19th-century building as the excellent Café Mindelo, it is decorated with ethnic artefacts and textiles. Guests have use of a small library, a computer connected to the internet, a kitchen and a rooftop barbecue.

Chez Loutcha €€ *Rua do Côco, Mindelo, tel: 232 1636.* This budget hotel has 29 old-fashioned but comfortable rooms; it's worth asking for one with a balcony as some are rather airless. The ground-floor restaurant is one of the best places in town to hear traditional music.

Foya Branca €€€ *São Pedro, tel: 230 7400,* www.foyabranca.com. For now, this is São Vicente's only beach hotel. Aircraft noise is occasionally a problem, but it has a relaxing atmosphere and a pleasant swimming pool area. Mindelo is 10 minutes away by free shuttle.

Mindelo Residencial €€ *Rua de Lisboa, Mindelo, tel: 230 0863, email:* m.residencial@gmail.com. Impeccably kept, this small, untouristy hotel has an unbeatable location right in the thick of things: the first- and second-floor balconies are great for people-watching. There's free Wi-fi, and breakfast is delicious.

Oásis Atlantico Porto Grande €€€ *Praça Nova, Mindelo, tel: 232 3190,* www.oasisatlantico.com. This, the island's most prestigious hotel, has rather uninspiring rooms but good facilities, including a swimming pool and gym. It's in a lively location, on Mindelo's sociable Praça Nova, and it is often used as a venue for special events.

Sodade €€ *Rua Franz Fanon 38, Mindelo, tel: 230 3200,* www.residencial sodade.com. A modest but well-run *residencial* with tidy rooms, some of which look out towards the bay – the higher the floor, the better the views. The spacious rooftop restaurant and terrace is a real bonus.

Villa St Aubyn €€ *Avenida de Fernando Ferreira Fortes 20, Mindelo, tel: 231 2725,* www.villastaubyn.com. Located in Mindelo's historic centre, Villa St Aubyn is a luxurious boutique hotel in a beautifully refurbished colonial-style house. It is also possible to rent the entire villa.

SANTO ANTÃO

Blue Bell €€ *Ponta do Sol, tel: 225 1215, email:* hotelbluebell@cvtele com.cv. A popular hotel in the centre of the small, pleasant town of Ponta do Sol, this has decent rooms with TV and distant views either of the sea or the mountains.

Casa Cavoquinho € *Chã de Manuel do Santos, Vale do Paúl, tel: 223 2065,* www.cavoquinho.com. This Spanish-owned guesthouse is perched high in the Paúl Valley, in a peaceful spot surrounded by inspiring hiking country. The owners can arrange transport and tours.

Mar Tranquilidade € *Tarrafal de Monte Trigo, tel: 227 6012, www.martranquilidade.com.* Well worth the two- or three-hour trip along the bumpy road from Porto Novo (if you can arrange it, arriving by boat is a good alternative), this tranquil retreat has simple thatched and tiled cottages on a beach of black sand.

Pedracin Village €€ *Boca de Coruja, tel: 224 2020.* In a remote but stunningly scenic location with panoramic views of the Ribeira Grande Valley and the craggy mountains beyond, this rural hotel consists of a clutch of traditional-style cottages in a garden of bougainvillea and aromatic shrubs, with a very pretty swimming pool.

Por do Sol Arte € *Ponta do Sol, tel: 225 1121, email:* porsolarte@yahoo.fr. With simple, fun rooms decked out in crazy colours, some featuring handmade log-frame beds, this is a characterful place to stay. It's right on the seafront, with a bar downstairs and other eateries nearby.

Santantão Art Resort €€–€€€ *Porto Novo, tel: 222 2675.* This is the island's first resort hotel, and also its largest, with 73 stylish, contemporary rooms and suites, a swimming pool and tennis court. It's on a black beach around 15 minutes' walk from town. The 'art' in the name refers to the display of works by local artists displayed in the lobby, all of which are for sale.

SÃO NICOLAU

Alice € *Rua de Praia, Tarrafal, tel: 236 1187.* This is a characterful *residencial*, situated right on Tarrafal's prettier bay, next to a small square where locals gather to chat and play *oril*.

Jardim € *Vila da Ribeira Brava, tel: 235 1117.* Up a steep slope at the southwest end of town, this friendly *pensão* has a top-floor terrace restaurant with views over the rooftops to the mountains beyond.

Santo António € *Vila da Ribeira Brava, tel: 235 2200, www.pensaosantoantonio.cv.* Overlooking the main square, this excellent *pensão* has bright, spotless rooms with TV, fridge and air conditioning. Breakfast is a feast of local cheese, ham, *cachupa*, bread and yogurt.

INDEX

Berlitz pocket guide

Cape Verde Islands

Second Edition 2015

Written by Emma Gregg
Updated by Magdalena Helsztynska
Edited by Rachel Lawrence
Cartography updated by Carte
Update Production: AM Services
Picture Editor: Tom Smyth
Production: Rebeka Davies and Aga Bylica

Photography credits: Dreamstime 87; Emma
Gregg/Apa Publications 1, 2TL, 2MC, 2TC, 2ML,
3T, 3TC, 3M, 3M, 3M, 3M, 4ML, 4ML, 4MR, 4TL,
4TL, 4/5M, 5MC, 4/5T, 5TC, 6TL, 6ML, 6ML,
7MC, 7MC, 7TC, 8, 10, 11, 12, 14, 16, 19, 20,
22, 26, 29, 31, 32, 35, 36, 37, 39, 40, 42, 44, 46,
47, 48, 49, 50, 52, 54, 55, 56, 57, 58, 59, 60, 61,
62, 63, 65, 67, 68, 69, 70, 71, 73, 74, 75, 77, 79,
81, 82, 84, 85, 86, 88, 89, 90, 92, 94, 95, 97, 98,
100, 102, 105; Getty Images 24; iStock 99; Mary
Evans Picture Library 15
Cover picture: AWL Images

Every effort has been made to provide
accurate information in this publication,
but changes are inevitable. The publisher
cannot be responsible for any resulting
loss, inconvenience or injury.

Contact us

At Berlitz we strive to keep our guides as
accurate and up to date as possible, but if you
find anything that has changed, or if you have
any suggestions on ways to improve this guide,
then we would be delighted to hear from you.

Berlitz Publishing, PO Box 7910,
London SE1 1WE, England.
email: berlitz@apaguide.co.uk
www.insightguides.com/berlitz